ENDORS

Just because God is speaking ~~~~~~~~~~~ ...ow it, and just because you know it, doesn't mean you automatically understand it.

We have to exercise the gift, develop the skill set and intentionally lean into God's prophetic voice by searching out the matter (Proverbs 25:2).

That is where this book comes in. *The King's Prophetic Voice* is a very helpful guide to train you to know when God is speaking, and what He is saying. I love this book.

God is speaking and revealing deep revelation knowledge through the common events going on around you, and through radical encounters He is inviting you into. The more you are willing to learn and respond to Him, the more you find how common, this uncommon, relationship can be.

Jodie Hughes is somebody who loves God's voice and is fascinated with the amazing heart of the Father. She lives in the beautiful tension between "a little girl" in joyous wonder and a fearless mighty warrior. Her book reflects this, and proves she is a next-level teacher, anointed to equip the saints.

I am honored to give this my highest endorsement. I can't wait to see the victories that will come from those who read it, and apply this insight to our lives.

TROY BREWER
Senior Pastor of Open Door Church
Founding Director of Troy Brewer
Ministries and Answer International
Author of *Redeeming your Timeline* and *Numbers that Preach*

Understanding and living by God's voice should be a top priority for every Christian. Jodie Hughes' book, *The King's Prophetic Voice*, will set you on fire with a holy passion to live every moment of every day by the voice of God and fill you with expectation of divine miracles at every turn of your life. I celebrate this book and encourage you to read it. This book can change your life.

Joan Hunter

Author/Healing Evangelist

Host of *Miracles Happen TV*

I remember the first time I heard one of Ben and Jodie's stories of God showing them repetitive numbers and I remember asking the Lord "Do you really speak like that?" It felt strange, yet wondrous, that He would choose to reveal His heart through the simple and the tangible. I began to long for it, look for it, and like a child start expecting to experience the full spectrum of Gods voice and language in a way I hadn't.

It wasn't much time later that I was in a crisis in my life, a crossroad that I didn't understand, and God began speaking to me in the same way He did with Ben and Jodie! It forever changed my life, gave me understanding, and made me feel fathered in a rough season.

I know that right now many feel detached from the Lord's heart because of the trials of life and the chaos in the world feels all consuming. Jodie's book, *The King's Prophetic Voice*, is a timely call to the simplicity, and discovery of the voice of the Lord, in this time of noise.

I pray this book awakens your ears so you can hear and your eyes so that you can see what you didn't before, and find yourself face to face with the King!

NATE JOHNSTON
Everyday Revivalists
Author of *The Wild Ones*

I remember the first time I ever heard God speak to me. I thought "Wow! I have access to the Creator of the entire universe?!" We can have a REAL relationship with Jesus, and that changes everything for us. So often Christians find themselves confused and wondering what God is doing.

I am so excited for Jodie Hughes' new book *The King's Prophetic Voice!* This is not just a vital message with practical teaching for EVERY believer, but I believe that we will see and experience greater harvest and revival if we can start paying attention to what God is doing on the earth.

Jodie is not only a trusted prophetic voice in our generation, but is a practitioner when it comes to searching out the deeper mysteries of God. So often I have found myself texting Jodie to interpret a dream, discover a prophetic pattern and risk on a vision for the sake of souls. Jodie is not only incredibly accurate with her prophetic insight, but she is a true friend of the King and one that I personally trust.

If you believe that there must be more and long to journey into treasure-filled fields of God's glory—then with urgency I suggest getting this book, putting on your seat belt, and preparing for the greatest adventure of your life! So long boring mundane days! The King is speaking!

JESSI GREEN
Revivalist, Saturate Global
Author of *Wildfires: A Field Guide to Supernatural Revival*

In *The King's Prophetic Voice*, Jodie Hughes takes you on a journey to discover hidden treasures from Heaven. Her prophetic insights will help you recognize that God is speaking to you all of the time in both ordinary and unusual ways, you might not have seen before. She not only helps you discover deeper revelation but she also equips you to hear God's voice and understand more clearly what He is speaking to you personally right now.

Jodie is a powerful and anointed woman of God who hears God's voice and acts. As you learn the secret ways of the King, may you encounter God's love in a profound way and commune with Him at a deeper level than ever before.

JENNIFER A. MISKOV, PH.D.
Founding Director of School of Revival
and Writing in the Glory
Author of *Fasting for Fire, Ignite Azusa* and more
JenMiskov.com

Wow! What a timely and helpful blessing this book is for the body of Christ. Understanding how to biblically interpret prophetic revelation is so important, and Jodie's new book is a powerful equipping tool to help Christians rightly steward the revelatory gifts. The blessing of hearing God's voice is the privilege of all God's children, and this book will greatly help you to become more aware and able to interpret what the Lord is saying to you.

Katherine Ruonala
Senior Leader
Glory City Church
Founder and Facilitator of the Australian Prophetic Council

For more than twenty years, as I've traveled around the world, I've been witness to the ways that the Spirit of God miraculously speaks to people through signs, wonders and divine symbolism. Although this spiritual phenomenon can often be tangibly felt and seen, the most important aspect of it is prophetic and spiritual in nature. There is a message in God's miracles and there is holy communication through His signs. I've observed that in general, when extraordinary supernatural things happen around most people, these things are only ignored simply because they are not understood. And for that reason, I am so thankful for this book and the timely message that Jodie Hughes shares through these pages.

It's time for God's people to wake up and hear and comprehend what the Heavenly King is decreeing! In her book, Jodie desires to teach God's people how to properly steward and decode the important prophetic revelations that are being delivered in this day through God's glory. I have been blessed to share ministry platforms with both Jodie and her husband Ben, and I can attest to the integrity and prophetic accuracy that they move in. *The King's Prophetic Voice* will challenge you to open your heart to the very heart of God, to understand and receive with clarity the prophetic message that He is sending directly to you. I highly recommend that you not only read this book, but pick up several copies and share them with your friends. This book is a true treasure from and for the Kingdom of glory.

JOSHUA MILLS,
International Speaker
Bestselling Author of *Moving in Glory Realms*
www.joshuamills.com

Many believers have wondered why the Lord often speaks in symbolism and seemingly fragmented revelations. Jodie Hughes, in *The King's Prophetic Voice*, offers profound insight and understanding into these ponderings, but also aids the reader in discerning, interpreting and understanding their own journey of prophetic discovery. Jodie is a seasoned and solid minister of the Word and the Lord's heart. I highly recommend her, and this book to you.

PATRICIA KING
Author, Minister, Media Producer

THE KING'S

PROPHETIC

VOICE

DESTINY IMAGE BOOKS BY JODIE HUGHES

The King's Decree:
Throne Room Declarations that Release
Supernatural Answers to Prayer

THE KING'S
PROPHETIC
VOICE

HEARING GOD SPEAK
THROUGH SYMBOLISM &
SUPERNATURAL SIGNS

JODIE HUGHES

DESTINY IMAGE® PUBLISHERS, INC.
P.O. Box 310, Shippensburg, PA 17257-0310

"Promoting Inspired Lives."

This book and all other Destiny Image and Destiny Image Fiction books are available at Christian bookstores and distributors worldwide.

For more information on foreign distributors, call 717-532-3040.

Reach us on the Internet: www.destinyimage.com.

ISBN 13 TP: 978-0-7684-6038-4
ISBN 13 eBook: 978-0-7684-6039-1
ISBN 13 HC: 978-0-7684-6041-4
ISBN 13 LP: 978-0-7684-6040-7

For Worldwide Distribution, Printed in the U.S.A.
1 2 3 4 5 6 7 8 / 26 25 24 23 22

DEDICATION

This book is dedicated to:

Jesus, who always talks and is never boring.

My husband, Ben, who always listens!

My Prophetic Avengers Book Club, with whom I have drunk a lot of coffee and processed *The King's Prophetic Voice* in many a dream, vision, and word. Thank you, Keely and Lauren.

A NOTE FROM JODIE

The King still speaks from burning bushes, small clouds, and rushing winds. His voice from within the fire still brands burning ones.

He is the door opener. The mystery revealer. And the God of Lazarus still.

The King has been writing Heaven's triumphs into your days from before you were born. His voice has been forging you, forming you, and loving you. He's been wooing you, leading you, and compelling you.

The Commander of Angel Armies has been calling you by name—with every whisper and roar He forged you as a sign and wonder of glory for the hour, chosen and sent from the Lord Almighty by utterance of the King's prophetic voice.

I bless you as a sign and wonder on the earth as you hear and obey *The King's Prophetic Voice*.

Jodie

Behold—here I stand, and the children whom the Lord Yahweh has given me are for signs and wonders in Israel, sent from the Lord Almighty, Commander of Angel Armies, who is enthroned on Mount Zion! (Isaiah 8:18 TPT)

FROM THE KING

The key of the house of David I [the Lord] will lay on his shoulder; so he shall open, and no one shall shut and he shall shut, and no one shall open (Isaiah 22:22 NKJV).

After he [Jesus] had said this, he went on to tell them, "Our friend Lazarus has fallen asleep; but I am going there to wake him up" (John 11:11 NIV).

I love you with an unrelenting love,
Listen for the sound of My voice.
The One who created you,
still calls you by name.

—THE KING

CONTENTS

FOREWORD

It was an absolute joy to meet Jodie Hughes and her husband, Ben, for the first time at GOD TV in Orlando, Florida. I had already observed their edgy and bold ministry endeavors on social media and enjoyed their posts that testified of God's power as they ministered and traveled.

They are true evangelists, having been sent from Australia by God to evangelize a desperate and unruly America, and have made a felt impact. As we chatted over lunch, I recognized Jodie's strong intercessory and prophetic nature and sensed a kindred spirit as we furthered along in our conversation.

You see, every prophetic intercessor has a history of remarkably answered prayer. They also cultivate a signature experience with His voice, something Jodie clearly demonstrates.

Our meeting day concluded after being interviewed in turn on the *Supernatural Life* show hosted by Patricia King. We were there with other prophets, revivalists, and authors who had been given the precious gift of media time to publicly share our unique teaching, testimonies, and newest books with the Body of Christ.

Jodie graciously invited me to pen the foreword of her latest book *The King's Prophetic Voice*. I'll add how it's the perfect sequel to her first book, *The King's Decree*. Hearing God's voice, seeing God's voice, and articulating what you see and hear with accuracy are some of my top pursuits as a leader in the global prophetic movement. I've immersed myself in these topics for most of my Christianity, having equipped and activated scores of prophets and thousands in the gift of prophecy.

To provide you with some background, my first encounter with His voice was just moments before I surrendered my life to Jesus. This was probably the second Christian church gathering that I had ever attended in my life, but I came to this meeting desperate. During the closing time of worship, Jesus spoke clearly to my heart. He didn't speak with words, but with a clearly identifiable thought, and I knew without a doubt that it was Him. He conveyed this to me, "I accept you just as you are." The impact of His voice was clear and exactly what I needed to go ahead and surrender my life to Him and never look back.

As I journeyed into my newly formed relationship with the Lord, I would experience His prophetic voice in ways that others had not heard of before, or even considered a possibility. I would hear His articulated voice within my heart and mind. I would see and sense His voice within my own being and through visions, dreams, divine coincidences, and in creation. This was happening to me and others like me long before anyone had developed instruction on social media, and prior to having access to solid books on the topic. If only I had a book like Jodie's when I began my journey with the creative voice of the Lord! It would have validated my experiences and helped me to run forward so much faster and with much less frustration.

This is why Jodie's book, *The King's Prophetic Voice*, is so important for us to lay hold of and read now. She allows us to see and experience her signature experience with God's multi-dimensional voice. Her book serves to fill in gaps of instruction in His voice that perhaps we've not heard of or considered before.

What stood out to me the most in Jodie's writings was her keen observation of God's prophetic voice playing out all around her in ways that many of us overlook, dismiss, or fail to notice. Jodie will cause you to look for His voice with a fresh set of eyes, while sharpening your vision to not miss what you've been missing up until now.

Additionally, her book is biblically sound (*hallelujah!*) and yet grows the capacity of your wineskin for more. She wrote this powerful truth, "He is the Word and He keeps speaking." With the help of her book, you will learn to not miss what He is saying.

JENNIFER EIVAZ
www.jennifereivaz.com
Co-Pastor of Harvest Church in Turlock, California
Founder, Harvest Ministries International
Author of *Seeing the Supernatural* and *Prophetic Secrets*

THE KING REVEALS MYSTERIES

He reveals the deep and hidden things,
he knows what lies in darkness, and
light dwells in him (Daniel 2:22 NIV).

K ING JESUS REVEALS SECRETS OF THE AGE AND WISDOM
for the everyday. To those who take the time to know Him
and recognize His voice, it's an adventure. God's voice has
been the rudder in my life's stormy times, and it has certainly
filled me with courage to step out and do things that initially I
thought were impossible.

At other times, His voice has made me laugh, mostly at
myself. I've definitely learned that God is not boring, and He
has a personality I've enjoyed getting to know! I can certainly
say that I've found God—through His voice in my life—to be
more loving, more holy, more creative, more "out of the box,"
and more playful than I ever imagined.

The God I know has surprised me at times with how He gets a message across. He doesn't seem to mind shocking me or smashing my ideas of what are "acceptable ways to hear God." I've sometimes thought I knew how He speaks, or more to the point, how He didn't speak—and time and time again God seems to have enjoyed blowing up my small thinking and expanding my idea of just how big He is, and also expanding my faith to live beyond my limitations.

What always astounds me though, is just how much God enjoys a good conversation and leading me into wisdom in ways that honestly make me smile and say, "Wow!" We all know that we are supposed to talk to Him through prayer, but it astounds me how much He likes to talk to us! He not only loves us, He likes us!

THE SUPERNATURAL IS NOT WEIRD TO GOD—IT'S HIS NORMAL.

There's no denying we are in extreme times of late, when people are desperate for hope and need the real God who shows up in real ways. As we navigate constantly shifting circumstances, the need for revelation from God in our daily lives is at the forefront of our prayers.

What I love about God is how "real" He is, constantly speaking into our places of need. The supernatural is not weird to God—it's His normal. In remembering that, we can see God for who He is and not miss the burning bushes, small clouds, and the rushing-wind moments laid up as treasure for our hearts.

As you read these pages, you will be ignited with childlike wonder and excitement for the season, adding hope where the world has only spoken gloom. You will find clarity as to your part in this season. God's prophetic voice is constantly leading us into our destiny and imparting the practical wisdom we need for the current times. He's also speaking to us as our heavenly Father who cares about our hearts. For this reason, sometimes He just wants to make you smile by saying, "I've got you, little one."

God Speaks Your Language

The Bible is our foundation, but we must remember that God isn't a textbook—He's the living God who speaks into our everyday. A living God, by definition, speaks! I never want to lose the joy or wonder of hearing God in my life, in what I term "common ways" including His Word the Bible; an inner, still small voice; or through any other way God chooses to speak and reveal a mystery of the eternal realm to me. I love His voice, even the out-of-the-box ways He leads me from mystery to message.

We need the living God in our midst, and we can't afford to miss recognizing what He's saying, especially in this season. We must grow greater discernment and focus on His voice and ways, if for no other reason than our children deserve this. May we leave them a legacy of a generation that recognizes when and how the King speaks.

If ever there was a season to be attuned to God's wisdom, I think we have found that season. We benefit from hearing

God through other people's voices, but hearing the voice of God for ourselves has never been more crucial.

This last season has served to highlight the need for razor-sharp clarity when it comes to hearing God and recognizing His prophetic voice and ways. Discerning the prophetic voice of the King in our own daily lives is one of the most life-giving tools we can have to navigate every season.

For too long, some have relegated the voice of God to only hearing Him through the Bible or the inner "still, small voice" (see 1 Kings 19:12 NKJV). This limited thinking steals the joy of real-time connection and communication with a very present and supernaturally active God. The King's prophetic voice is current and continually active, helping us not turn to the "left or the right," but to hear which way to go (see 2 Kings 22:2; 2 Chronicles 34:2; Isaiah 30:21 NKJV).

The thing is, many of us are hearing God speak in all manner of creative and unusual ways, just like He did in the Bible. The key is recognizing and translating the King's prophetic voice and ways alongside the Word of God as our foundation.

Sometimes while reading the Bible, the prophetic symbolism, supernatural signs, and divine encounters that appear constantly in its pages can be almost overlooked. Yet I believe God wants us to expect His supernatural power to break in as we go about our daily lives and fulfill our part in the great commission! God reveals through Scripture that He is infinitely greater than the limitations of this world, and vastly more powerful than the best the enemy can come up with—and He wants us to see this written into the pages of His Word.

More than Historical Stories

The stories of the Bible should stir us, not just as a record of history, but as an invitation into relational connection with the most glorious Being, who speaks with unending creativity. Let's not forget we serve the God who speaks from the burning bush, Balaam's donkey, and through Gideon's fleece. *"The heavens declare the glory of God"* (Psalm 19:1 NKJV), and angels sing "Holy, holy, holy!" (Isaiah 6:3 KJV). He spoke through dreams to Mary, Joseph, Daniel, and even King Nebuchadnezzar, a secular leader.

Angels announced the birth of the Lord as seen by shepherds, and an angel of the Lord told Mary, the mother of Jesus, that she would give birth to the Messiah. An angel spoke to Gideon, Abraham, and Zechariah. Ezekiel had visions of "wheels within a wheel." The disciple John had prophetic visions of the future. The disciple Peter had a vision in Acts 10 that changed the church of the day and instructed the preaching of the gospel to Gentiles. Elijah saw a small cloud, fire fall from Heaven, ran faster than a chariot, and an angel fed him when he was exhausted. Isaiah speaks of the still small voice.

In Acts 2, the Holy Spirit ministers as a mighty rushing wind. In Exodus, hailstones fall on enemy troops, and the sun stands still to provide time for greater defeat of the enemy in Joshua. The Bible gives us much reason to compel us to know a very creative God who speaks in very supernatural ways.

I read these Bible stories and I'm stirred to an uncommon pursuit to know this King who speaks and "all who came to Him were healed" (Matthew 8:16), and whose voice still calls "fishermen" to be nation changers.

While following along this path of hearing God speak to me, I have learned to pay attention. I know that every time God has shown me something miraculous, unusual, or mystical, He's been growing my faith to believe in the impossible and fulfill my call. He's doing the same for you.

We're all called to a revival lifestyle and to fulfill the great commission. Faith for the impossible is not just a nice concept, it is an essential tool for living in these times. Every encounter is building and forging in us strength and trust in the God who still parts "red seas" for our families and can build or destroy a nation in a day. Every time He speaks, He is giving us courage to rise up and shine right where we are.

God Is Still Speaking

The shakings and storms are not the story right now, but rather what Heaven is declaring over you. What is God's strategy for you? What is God's voice stirring in you? As you hear God, you will be stirred to believe for the unseen and the unheard, yet mighty exploits on earth. Revelation increases as you carve out new paths into uncharted territory.

For instance, faith to see entire hospitals cleared out and every patient healed in a moment isn't forged without faith in the God who still turns the impossible to possible. God's prophetic interactions with us are reminders of His power beyond the circumstances we face. As we partner with God's voice of hope, we grow in authority to move mountains in our lives. This is why we need to understand the burning bush, small clouds, and rushing-wind encounters in our lives today. He's reminding us that He is still powerful; we have a Deliverer, and He is with us!

Just how He speaks to you, my friend, God is speaking to people worldwide, sometimes through visions or a strange encounter or a sign that blows their mind and makes them wonder. These prophetic signs are not beyond understanding—they are signposts to Jesus and direction for navigating well in uncertain times.

I am compelled to emphasize again that the Bible is our foundation, and nothing God does or says will diminish or violate the supremacy of His Word. To love God is to love His Word and desire to read it and apply it to our lives. Second Timothy 3:16 (NIV) says, *"All Scripture is God-breathed and useful for teaching, rebuking, correcting and training in righteousness."* Therefore, the entirety of the Bible is inspired by God and must be honored as such.

I am equally compelled to highlight that the Bible compels and implores us to know God in all His ways. God is the Creator of the universe who continues to speak to His people in creative, experiential, and prophetically symbolic ways. The creativity of the King didn't end in the days of Genesis.

As we journey together through *The King's Prophetic Voice*, you will discover the key to how God speaks in "normal" *and* prophetic ways. You will also discover why God talks through supernatural signs, wonders, and encounters, what is He saying, and why He would say it that way.

Supernatural Language Symbolism

The church and the harvest fields are full of people who have experienced God speaking through unusual phenomena and prophetic symbolism, just as He did in the Bible. The supernatural voice of God should not be relegated to the back rooms or supposed "super spiritual" conferences, streams or denominations. Maturity of faith, character, holiness, fear of the Lord, and biblical soundness go hand in hand with the language of the Spirit and supernatural encounters. The supernatural, prophetic voice of God is both normal and biblical.

God speaks supernatural language and symbolism fluently, and He is constantly speaking through His prophetic voice in this way, to break us out of stale, lifeless, and powerless religion. Thankfully, the prophetic has been normalized in much of the church, but we must also normalize encountering and receiving from the King's prophetic voice—even when it is mysterious, symbolic, or supernatural. In doing so, we bring solid scriptural foundations to God speaking supernaturally and validate the ways God is speaking to the harvest and many around us all the time.

People all around the world are having dreams, visions, angelic encounters, hearing God through nature, and having supernatural experiences such as gold dust appearing or feathers manifesting. Many smell fragrances or awaken to songs being sung over them that they "hear in their spirit." Many are repetitively seeing the same numbers over and over such as 11:11 or 22:22 or 911, to the point it's driving them to desperation to understand what God is saying. Some constantly hear fire alarms or bells ringing or trumpet sounds in the spirit.

Some see pictures of people and nations drop in front of them that come with an urgency to pray. Many feel pain in their body that is not their own, or flames suddenly appear in front of them as they worship, or a glory cloud, or have felt supernatural rain falling indoors. Others see angels, dream vivid dreams they swear are real, or hear the echoes of God's voice through simple conversations with their children. God speaks many different ways, but supernatural is His normal.

If you have heard God speak in such ways, or wondered why would He talk through symbols or mysterious ways that require interpretation, I speak joy to your heart as we set out on this journey together. Conversation with God was never meant to be dull and lifeless. God is the most creative Communicator and present Conversationist in the universe. Why would we think that how He speaks to us personally today would be anything less than creative and full of life?

May I kindly say that we can make the mistake of assuming that if someone doesn't have constant supernatural encounters and "mystical manifestations," that this person is a less-mature spiritual believer than someone who is always having wild, supernatural encounters and mystical manifestations. That assumption is not true. The number of encounters we have is not the point—our response is important. No particular way God speaks is more elite or special than another way. The point is that God speaks! His prophetic voice activates faith we need to walk in His message to us.

Be ignited in your hunger after God. Recognizing His voice in the multiple ways He speaks changes everything. Destiny is

13

found in discerning and translating the King's prophetic voice already in your midst.

The Mystical Becomes a Message as We Translate His Voice

You may have had experiences that you thought were strange, too weird, or outside your paradigm of how God speaks. Perhaps you knew it was God speaking, despite being unusual, and you are seeking wisdom to interpret its meaning in a solid, pro-supernatural, and scriptural way. In the translation of His prophetic voice, we turn the mystical into the message.

Perhaps you have so many encounters or supernatural experiences that it's overwhelming and you need simple keys to deciphering what is going on. Maybe you know God is speaking to you but you've felt confused, misunderstood, or need keys to break off demonic torment in these areas and find peace as you hear His supernatural voice.

Every encounter you have is intended to amplify Jesus in your life and remind you of God's love and power.

UNDERSTANDING GOD'S VOICE IS NOT PRIMARILY AN INTELLECTUAL PURSUIT, RATHER IT IS A PURSUIT OF RELATIONSHIP.

My journey hearing the King's prophetic voice has taught me that experiencing the supernatural language of the Spirit is living a supernaturally normal lifestyle. It has also taught me to value childlike faith, and that translating encounters is not intended to be beyond the reach of every child of God.

I value resources such as biblical dream interpretation guides and prophetic teaching, which I use to grow in wisdom. I very much appreciate the Strong's Concordance to study the origin of words and symbols, and I enjoy researching the Hebrew meaning of different numbers and words. But I want to communicate something very clearly—understanding God's voice is not primarily an intellectual pursuit; but rather, the primary pursuit is one of relationship. It's not about formula, but friendship with God.

There is nothing like the adventure of discovering that the King of the universe sent you a personal message. It charges your insides with tangible hope! For this reason, the King's prophetic voice is vehemently warred against by the enemy. Speaking with prophetic insight and authority into current circumstances in your own life, or the nations, is dangerous to the devil. The enemy would rather have God's people live in perpetual confusion, fogginess, and apathy, hearing but never understanding God's word and prophetic wisdom. That day is over though. The King's prophetic voice is roaring over His people.

Understanding the King's prophetic voice is more simple, and yet more profound than you may have thought, more fun than you imagined, and more needed than ever. Our God talks and does so with such beauty and wonder. The King's prophetic voice calls you from the burning bush to days of destiny.

Grab a pen. Grab a coffee.

Here we go, my friend.

The King's prophetic voice awaits.

Part One

RECOGNIZING THE KING'S PROPHETIC VOICE

Thus says the Lord, who created you..."I have called you by your name; you are Mine" (Isaiah 43:1 NKJV).

1

GOD SPEAKS YOUR LANGUAGE

Thus says the Lord, who created you..."I have called you by your name; you are Mine" (Isaiah 43:1 NKJV).

I BELIEVE EVERYONE WANTS TO HEAR GOD. HOWEVER, REC-ognizing His prophetic voice in our everyday lives is the key to hearing His voice.

The learning process of deciphering the prophetic voice and the ways God speaks in our lives is the "x marks the spot" treasure of the hunt. The treasure is access to hear the very voice of God and wisdom from the glory realm! This is mind-blowing if you think about it long enough. But what is even more mind-blowing is knowing that the One who created us calls us personally by name into destiny and gives us road maps to get there.

God not only wants to talk to us, He is chasing us down—and He is very good at the chase! Our God who created the universe is more intelligent than we can even imagine, and is a masterful Communicator, fluent in speaking every person's language. God knows your name and is talking to you in ways you *can* understand.

"Your word is a lamp to my feet and a light to my path" (Psalm 119:105 NKJV). We need God's word to illuminate the roads on which we travel.

Psalm 139:16 (TPT) tells us, *"You [God] saw who you created me to be before I became me! Before I'd ever seen the light of day, the number of days you planned for me were already recorded in your book."* And verse 5 says, *"You've gone into my future to prepare the way...."* Verse 11 is profound, *"It's impossible to disappear from you [Lord] or to ask the darkness to hide me, for your presence is everywhere, bringing light into my night."* His word is a light to my feet, and a lamp to my path that shines *"light into my night."* Or in other words, when you feel alone when facing the challenges of life, His presence and voice is with you. His voice calls to the deepest part of you, and it always has.

Let's take a moment though and remind ourselves how amazing it is that God is relational, and therefore initiates speaking to us personally, and giving us road maps to follow all the days of our life. I often imagine a moment something like this as God created us, when God knew us before we were born and breathed life into us: I can see Him in my mind's eye as the heavenly Father, tenderly whispering over us in that moment, "Precious one, remember My voice. I love you with an unrelenting love, and I'll be here with you. Listen for the sound of My voice."

And so the most inner part of us has been searching and listening for the sound of His voice ever since.

John 10:27 (NKJV) says, *"My sheep hear My voice."* You hear Him. Your heavenly Father who made you has been speaking to you all your life, whether you recognized Him or not. His voice continues to communicate with you in ways that resonate in the innermost part of you, because He made you. We grow in understanding, but the truth remains—your spirit was made to hear your heavenly Father.

The exhilarating adventure is discovering that God speaks our language, *your* language to be specific. He doesn't make you learn some foreign language, earn a six-year doctorate in theology, or study biblical Hebrew to speak to Him. He simply speaks *your* language! Think about that. God speaks your language because He made you and understands every thought before it even enters your mind. He is intimately aware of you. God knows how to reach out to you and speak in ways that connect to your heart.

> *...How thoroughly you know me, Lord! You even formed every bone in my body when you created me in the secret place; carefully, skillfully you shaped me from nothing to something. You saw who you created me to be before I became me!* (Psalm 139:14-16 TPT)

Remembering God's Voice

Recognizing God's interactions in our lives and hearing Him with greater clarity is, of course, wisdom. Largely, that's what this book is about! But let's start with the truth that hearing God is simple and not intended to be complicated. God knows what makes you tick and He knows the language of your heart. Hearing God is not an exercise in intellectualism, but rather the action of cultivating a friendship and learning the nuances of the heart of God. I like to think of it as "remembering God's voice." He is the One who breathed life into you, the One who can read your heart like an open book, the One who created you and calls you by name.

> *You perceive every movement of my heart and soul, and you understand my every thought before it even enters my mind. You are so intimately aware of me, Lord. You read my heart like an open book and you know all the words I'm about to speak before I even start a sentence!* (Psalm 136: 2-3 TPT)

God talks through His written Word, the Bible, and also through His spoken prophetic voice. When you hear God speak in either way, it cuts through the noise and adds needed divine wisdom into our lives.

Recognizing the "spoken" prophetic voice of God in your life and realizing that God is speaking directly to you is beyond exhilarating.

Defining the Prophetic Voice of God

For purposes of this book, I define the prophetic voice of God as any way God speaks to us through His spoken, creative word. It's the *rhema* word of God, which is the Greek word for "utterance," or "thing said," defined as the spoken word of God.

Specifically, God's prophetic voice is when He speaks directly, individually or corporately, through an inner witness to our spirit through signs, wonders, the miraculous, the super-natural, and prophetic symbolism. That covers a lot of ways God can speak, and I want to keep the definition broad, remembering that God talks to us all individually in ways that are personal to each of us.

I'm cautious about "over-defining" how He speaks, as God's voice is a living, ongoing, personal and individual conversation. And no matter how He speaks, you will know His voice reso-nating inside you, and drawing you to Jesus.

To be practical though, there are similarities in how God speaks including dreams, visions, angelic encounters, visita-tions in dreams, eyes-open visions, supernatural experiences, and prophetic symbolism where God highlights something in the natural to release a spiritual message.

There's more! Take a breath as I mention some other exam-ples of ways people can hear God:

- Waking up at the same time every night for weeks.
- "Seeing" the same number sequence over and over.
- Hearing sounds in your spirit like angels singing or alarms going off.
- Manifestations from the glory realm such as feathers or diamonds.
- Suddenly smelling fragrance such as roses or something sweet.
- Feeling God's pleasure.
- Hearing His laughter.

- Seeing scrolls, maps or blueprints of designs or inventions appear in front of you.
- Seeing something that you know was not natural but from the heavenly realm.
- Hearing God's voice through nature, thunder for instance, or animals, rainbows or sunsets.

Breathe again, there are more examples:

- Sensing God speak though your children, a movie, or sermon.
- Experiencing a trance or sudden vision.
- Feeling as if you are actually in another place and prompted to pray.
- Receiving a word through a painting or song.
- Seeing the same car license plate till it drives you crazy.
- Hearing God's audible or inner voice.
- Bible verses flashing past your mind's eye.
- Seeing clouds in worship, or fire, or colors.
- Waking up to hearing a song sung over you.
- Seeing a vision of Jesus.
- Hearing heavenly music.
- Waking up and immediately seeing a picture in your spirit or knowing something from God for the day.
- Experiencing anything supernatural and beyond earthly reasoning.

THE PROPHETIC VOICE OF GOD IS INDEED PROPHETIC AND PERSONAL.

The prophetic voice of the King is a living utterance; therefore it is personal, prophetically creative, and supernatural.

These few examples of God's voice through prophetic symbolism and creative utterance are far from an exhaustive list—though I laugh as I write that because it may seem exhausting! My purpose in giving examples is for you to immediately recognize some of these ways God speaks to you, or to expand your understanding. Every one of the examples I listed are ways God has used in my life to speak to me, or the lives of people I minister to who are looking for help to discern what is happening. And each of these ways God speaks are more common than most think.

I assure you we are going to look at this important topic with biblical wisdom, and with our discernment turned on.

As we established though, God speaks your language! That means He knows you, and so the prophetic symbolism He uses in your life is often unique to you, so it's understood by you.

God's Prophetic Voice in the Bible Was Normal

God speaks through His prophetic voice throughout the Bible with signs and wonders, angelic visitations, unusual supernatural manifestations or experiences, dreams and visions, and prophetic symbolism to mention just a few ways. Each time God spoke, it created a moment of the glory realm intersecting our earthly realm to deliver a message that carried heavenly wisdom. Or put simply, God interrupted people's lives and got their attention.

I know some can get nervous when discussing signs like this, but let me assure you, it's clear in the Bible that this is a normal way God communicated with people.

Received and Remembered

I specifically think of the birth of Jesus. God was very busy communicating through angels what people needed to hear in ways that ensured the message was received and remembered. An angel told Mary in an open-eye encounter the life-changing news about becoming pregnant supernaturally with God's Son. The dad-to-be, Joseph, had a dream in which an angel gave him peace about marrying Mary, which was highly unusual and beyond the logic and practice of the day. The message was indeed from God. Angels appeared to shepherds at night and a star in the sky led influential truth seekers right to Jesus. Later in another dream, Mary and Joseph saved Jesus' life by being obedient to its message and was the catalyst for their family to not just move their home, but move nations. Then in yet another dream years later, details and timing of moving nations again are given, and Mary, Joseph, and baby Jesus pack up their lives and begin a new season again. A lot of crucial information given by angelic encounters, signs and in dreams. I'm glad they paid attention and didn't consider God's voice as just a strange "pizza" dream or weird, unimportant encounter.

God is leading you in the same way He led the parents of His Son—with great love, speaking personally and prophetically into your life.

What We Steward Grows

As you read this book, I know you're excited and eager for more. Perhaps you already have a grid for the prophetic voice of God and simply hunger to understand more clearly how God is intercepting your world with His voice. I know this—what we steward grows. So as we steward God's voice in our lives, God brings the increase. Expect the increase! I'm excited for you to have heightened clarity, revelation, and hunger in your life as you pursue all that God is saying to you.

No wonder the devil wants to make it seem so difficult or so "fringe" to hear God specifically and supernaturally, when in reality it's simple and biblical. God is a supernatural God; and when He speaks in supernatural ways, He is speaking the language of the Spirit directly to us. Again, to avoid pitfalls, the Bible is our guidebook.

GOD SPEAKS YOUR HEART LANGUAGE.

The Supernatural Sparks Curiosity

God will use curiosity in our journeys to draw us to Jesus. In fact, that is often the purpose of God using His supernatural voice, for instance the sound of a "rushing wind."

Acts 2 describes Pentecost when the disciples are filled with the Holy Spirit for the first time, and spilled out of the upper room and into the city. The Bible says, *"When the people of the city heard the roaring sound, crowds came running to where it was coming from, stunned over what was happening, because each one could hear the disciples speaking in his or her own language"* (Acts

2:6 TPT). The Holy Spirit is still using His prophetic voice to draw a crowd.

Tongues of fire that looked like flames hovered over the disciples' heads, (imagine seeing that), and they were filled with the Holy Spirit and began speaking in other tongues, other languages. The crowd of people gathered were from "every nation" the Bible says, (meaning representatives from every single nation at the time), and they were suddenly *drawn* by the supernatural sound. The Bible says they were all "utterly amazed" at what they saw and heard next.

They knew the disciples were Galileans, yet everyone in the diverse crowd from different nations heard the disciples speaking in their own native language! Think about that. The crowd of many nationalities all heard the wonders of God being declared in their own language! Clearly they somehow knew something strange was happening because they asked, *"Aren't all these who are speaking Galileans? Then how is it that each of us hears them in our native language?"* (Acts 2:7-8 NIV). They said out loud, *"what does this mean?"* (Acts 2:12 NIV) That reminds me of an often common response when God does something strange our lives, "What does this mean?"

Some, of course, mocked this amazing miracle and accused the disciples all of being drunk with wine, similar to what some say about God's people today who have supernatural encounters and are mocked. But the Bible also says that many were so impacted by what they heard that they became believers that very day! Acts 2:41 tells us that 3,000 *"were added to their number that day."* Take note, the supernatural signs that day sparked curiosity and led people to Jesus!

God Spoke Each Person's Language

But let me highlight a truth to you that is often missed. Before Peter preached the famous first sermon in Acts 2, after being filled with the Holy Spirit power and anointing, the crowd was already hearing about God in their own native language. The crowd consisted of Jews and converts to Judaism, those who believed in God, and those who had heard Jesus or stories about Him while He was walking the earth only days ago.

There were also those there who were clearly not believers—people who were unsaved, unchurched, regular people just going about their day in the city. All the people together miraculously and suddenly heard the message of God's wonder and goodness in a way they could understand. It arrested them and interrupted their day. God ensured that in that moment, everybody—the godly and the ungodly—supernaturally heard clearly from God, as the disciples were astoundingly speaking multiple languages all at once. And the crowd didn't just hear, they understood. God spoke their language directly to them, letting them know they were seen and loved by God. The godly and the ungodly heard the supernatural voice of God.

God still does this. He speaks everybody's language. He knows how to speak to your heart, arrest your attention, and open your eyes to the wonders of the Almighty. In this incredible language miracle that happened the day the church was birthed, God was also ensuring that we—all these centuries later—understand that He still sees and loves us, and knows *how* to communicate with us personally in ways we will understand. He knows how to speak our language and ensure we understand His voice.

This is a great biblical precedent for my next point that will encourage you greatly, friend!

God's Calling Card

God knows how to speak specifically to your family and friends and all those you are praying for. He speaks in ways they understand to provoke them to open their spiritual eyes—often in supernatural ways. The King's prophetic voice still interrupts, intercepts, and knows how to speak every person's specific language.

If God has to break in through a dream, He will! If He has to keep waking someone up at 11:11 p.m. every night for a month until they ask what it means, He will. If God has to speak to their fearful heart through an encounter they can't explain, He will. God still uses "prophetic rushing winds" to birth curiosity and create a hunger for Jesus. God speaks everybody's language!

Be encouraged as you pray that God is already talking and priming hearts with curiosity, preparing them to know Him personally. The Holy Spirit still draws people to Jesus.

God is speaking to people who aren't "saved" yet. This we may know, but it's good to remember, as the harvest comes in, many are looking for understanding of the God who has already been supernaturally drawing them through "rushing winds" to His heart. Let's not sell God short to them. Let's not give them a textbook God, but a God who speaks supernaturally still.

God's calling card is the supernatural. He still taps on hearts in ways that "astound and perplex" (Acts 2:12) people still. God knows how to reach people. He speaks their language still.

While on this topic, let me join my faith with yours and pray for your loved ones who need an encounter with Jesus' saving grace.

Pray this prayer with me:

> *Holy Spirit, I thank You that You know our loved ones because You created them, and so we pray right now that You would move on their hearts, speak to them, and call them by name to You. We cry out on behalf of our loved one (name them individually _____) and we pray for them to find peace in You, to receive Your invitation of Your love into salvation and eternal security found only in You, Jesus. We pray they discover their call in You. We call them into encounters of Your love, and supernatural power and presence. We rebuke the enemy over their life trying to shut their spiritual hearing and we bless their ears to hear, their eyes to see, and their hearts to know You, Jesus, in the fullness of Your glory. We decree they will serve You, Lord, and walk in the days they were born to live. We bless their hearts to hear, see and know You, Jesus. We call in angels on assignment to them, and dreams and encounters that speak directly to their hearts, arresting their attention to Your wonder and righteousness. Lord, we say, here I am use me, and we make ourselves available to partner with in prayer for them, and do*

*anything practical You would like us to. In the name
of our King Jesus, amen.*

Amen and amen. Be expectant, friend. God loves them,
and He loves you.

The Enemy Wars Against the Prophetic Voice of God

We live in a time when the voice of God is needed, but His
voice is constantly being warred against, now more than ever.
There is so much confusion, noise, and chaos around us—yet
hearing God's voice brings peace, wisdom, and direction to our
actual circumstances. Hearing God brings clarity as we evict
distractions and focus on His higher truth. This is exactly why
the enemy wars against our relationship with God and tries
to prevent us from maturing in our faith. The prophetic voice
of God says you are seen and known. No wonder the devil
wants to make life seem so difficult. God is supernatural and
He speaks in supernatural ways; He speaks the language of the
Spirit directly to us.

The enemy has been very busy making people feel isolated
and alone, or making them think God doesn't see them personally or care what's going on. The prophetic voice of the
King is maligned, mocked, misunderstood, and attacked by
religious devils.

God is speaking directly to you though. He cares about
the big things and the little things. He's communicating and
speaking your language with words of life that resonate to the
deepest part of who you are. God knows how to make you
smile, pay attention to something important, and reach your

heart with His hope and wisdom. Not only that, He knows how to ensure that what He says impacts your heart, not just your head. More than any good earthly parent, our heavenly Father knows and understands your heart language and loves to declare *"the wonders of God"* directly to you (see Acts 2:11 NIV).

A word from God—the King's prophetic voice for you today:

> I have always been after your heart. I've always been there, always wooing you, and speaking promise over you. You are born with a sense of destiny, as I put Heaven's promises in your heart before you were born. I've been speaking destiny over you ever since, and capturing your attention to remind you that you're loved. It's always been about pointing you to Jesus, and building confidence in you that I believe in you—the "God dream" in you that drives you. I am actively growing faith in you to arise and fulfill. The enemy has tried to snuff out your passion and convince you breakthrough will never come, but I am greater than the world and all the enemy can throw at you. My voice has always beckoned you, drawn you, and compelled you to believe for more. I desire friendship with you, My child. I am growing your capacity and clarity to hear and know My voice and My ways. Trust Me. I'm with you and leading you. Look for the breath of My Spirit in your everyday, even if it's different from what you expect. I am with you

and leading you with My voice from weariness to wonder, and into new territory of promise fulfilled.

—THE KING

The One who created you has also been actively engaged in drawing you to His heart and stretching you to believe the dreams He placed in your heart. Sometimes it's His still small voice, sometimes a rushing wind, sometimes a burning bush. But always, the prophetic voice of the King compels you to believe in Him for more.

I bless every way God is speaking to your heart, and I bless you to marvel in this truth; it's never been just about a dream or wild encounter or prophetic sign that gripped your heart. It's always been about the One who called you by name saying, "I believe in you." Let's believe Him for even more.

The most important question I can ask you:

Maybe you have never said yes to Jesus as Lord and Savior of your life, or maybe you are just realizing as you read this that it's time to reconnect your heart fully to God. If you're the latter, simply pray, "Jesus, I surrender all of my life to You, and I choose to live wholeheartedly for You, fully embracing all You are saying to me, and running hard after You."

Amen, friend, and bless you.

If however, you've never said yes to Jesus, it's time, friend. You may know about God, but it's time to actually *know* God personally. His voice has been speaking to you for a long time, and you know this as your heart is pounding right now that something inside you is coming alive and recognizing the heartbeat of Heaven calling you "home." You're loved, friend, and it's time to reply to the invitation of His love. It's time to say, "Yes, Jesus, I hear You calling me." Simply pray this with me:

> *Jesus, I invite You into my heart and life as Lord and Savior. Thank You for calling me. Thank You for chasing after my heart. I receive Your love for me. Please forgive me for my sins. I receive Your forgiveness, God, and I thank You for Your grace. Fill me with Your presence, God. Fill me with Your power. I receive Your Holy Spirit to come make a home in me, and empower me to live my life for You. I thank You that I will increasingly hear Your voice in my life, and I'm excited to discover more. I thank You that my name is now written in the Lamb's Book of Life, and I will spend eternity with You when I pass from this life into Heaven. In Jesus' name, amen.*

And Amen from me too friend! God bless you.

P.S. You'll enjoy the book a whole lot more now! I bless you as you read.

Mentoring Moment with the King

These mentoring questions have no right or wrong answers. They are designed to provoke thought and reflection, help you summarize your experience and expectations, and promote growth as you explore your journey with God's prophetic voice. Be honest and real.

- God's voice is personal and individual. What are the most common ways God speaks to you?

- Remember a time God made you feel loved and seen, and thank Him for His voice.

- When is a time God has used something "out of the box" to speak to you?

- What is God stirring fresh faith in you for? How is He doing that?

- Is there a God dream that He is asking you to pick back up, or a new dream He is speaking to you about?

- What encounters have you had lately that have increased your faith for this current season?

- What we steward, grows. What is one way you are stewarding your relationship with God and what God is saying to you in this season?

- Take a moment and thank God for the times He has spoken to you and pointed you to Jesus. How has this impacted your life?

Activation Prayer

Lord, I ask for increased hunger to hear You in all Your ways in my life. Amen.

2

FROM MYSTICAL
TO MESSAGE

N OW LET'S DELVE INTO THE VERY PERSONAL PURPOSE OF
the King's prophetic voice.

I'll never forget some years back going through a very
tough season that felt like it would never end. My lifeline was
the very personal prophetic voice of God.

In the wee early hours one morning, in my prayer room
God spoke to me in the quiet. When I couldn't sleep because
of worries and the stress of trying to work out how to navigate
a painful season, I'd get up and pray. Sometimes my praying
looked more like just sitting with God in the realness of the
stuff with tears in my eyes, and watching in the dark, expec-
tantly waiting for first light to break through the horizon. God
was using the sunrise to speak hope into me day after day.

Watching the dawn break every morning spoke an inexpli-
cable hope to my soul. One day I clearly heard Him say, "The
light is beginning to break, Jodie, just like dawn breaks through
the darkness every morning." I'll never forget that morning.

The sunrise itself seemed to prophesy, "This season is shifting, Jodie; just as the sunlight pierces through, I am breaking through for you." I have tears writing this, because I remember the struggle and pain of that season, and I remember the hope and courage that sunrise prophesied to me. It may have been just a sunrise to others, but to me it was the very personal prophetic voice of my King.

Truly, *"The heavens declare the glory of God; the skies proclaim the work of His hands"* (Psalm 19:1 NIV).

I sometimes wondered why God didn't speak the first morning I watched for the light to arise. But I came to realize that the season of night watch, or dawn watch, became the prophetic word in itself when I saw first light every day. I needed to wait and "see" the light break through. I needed to "see" the heavens declare and prophesy.

DISCOVERING THE PURPOSE OF HIS VOICE HELPS US UNDERSTAND THE LANGUAGE HE USES.

To discern the message of God's prophetic voice to us, recognizing the purpose often helps bring understanding to the symbolism used. For instance, a dream about warfare is often a call to intercession, or God training us in the night hours for the season ahead. The images represent a battle in the spirit, and the emotions from the dream are purposed to evoke urgency to pray. When you understand God is good, even a call to prayer is His goodness, as we pray from victory, not for victory, with the added advantage of prophetically strategic insight.

A Personal Message from God to You

The dream, sign, or encounter is a message from God. The message could simply be, "It's time to pray," "I love you and see you," or purposefully designed to increase your faith or give specific direction. Either way, the King is sending a message through His prophetic voice, and it is personal for you.

If the purpose is to encourage you, receive it as encouragement. If the purpose is to stretch your faith, receive it as keys for growth. If the purpose is to provide insight into a situation you're facing, receive it as wisdom. There may be multiple meanings, but often we know if something is revelation, encouragement, a call to prayer, or for the purpose of insight. Ask yourself, *What is the purpose of this?* Answering that question will help you understand the mystical and unlock the message.

Don't Overcomplicate the Message

Sometimes we have a propensity to overcomplicate things in our journey with God. God is and has always been the God who speaks. As our heavenly Father, He's also invested in our heart; and many times God is speaking to us simply as the Father who loves us. Sometimes there's no deeper meaning than for Him to say, "You are loved." There is often more revelation in the encounter to come, but don't overlook the personal message of love. For instance, gold dust can be a sign of His glory realm breaking in, or the atmosphere is charged for the miraculous, but it's also a miraculous sign and message of God's love for you. Don't miss the profound, simple message in the encounter when searching out the mystical.

NOT OVERCOMPLICATING THE SIMPLICITY OF THE PROPHETIC VOICE OF THE KING UNLOCKS THE MESSAGE FROM THE MYSTICAL.

The first time I saw gold dust, I felt so very loved by God. Gold dust is literally gold manifesting supernaturally, often on people's skin. I was overwhelmed with thankfulness to Jesus, and seeing it also exponentially grew my faith. I didn't need to fully understand, I just knew my heart was charged with wonder and childlike faith for Jesus.

Years ago, I was in hospital in a desperate way medically speaking; I had been in isolation for about four weeks, which was far from fun. One evening I had been sitting up praying for hours, as the pain was intense and my situation was dire—but my hope was in God and His word. As I got back into bed and began to drift off to sleep, I suddenly "saw" golden light stream into my hospital room, and floating within the golden beam of light were hundreds of tiny gold dust particles. My eyes were open. I wasn't asleep. It was beautiful. It was mystical. It was glorious. The atmosphere was suddenly charged with God's presence. I watched the golden beam of light move across the room till it settled on me, and the golden cloud swirled gently around me. I was in awe. I felt my faith surge. Eventually it disappeared, but the peace of God remained.

I could overanalyze this, as it was an unusual encounter with my eyes open. But I knew it was God. I felt His presence so tangibly, and childlike faith arose. I've since studied the meaning of gold in the Bible and read about its connection to glory; but in that moment, the simple message of the encounter was that God was with me. I was in a hospital room with no real medical hope, and this was my King Jesus sending me a personal message, "I'm with you, Jodie." My faith certainly increased.

I eventually fell asleep, and then awoke to what I thought was a nurse's hand on my arm. When I opened my eyes there was no nurse there, but I could feel a hand on my arm still. Again, I knew God was simply saying, "I'm with you, Jodie, and I love you." My healing was fast-forwarded and accelerated recovery took place, enough that I was released from hospital in time to go home and attend my daughter's ninth birthday party. Jesus is good, and His mystical ways deliver very personal messages to us.

Relationship Unlocks Revelation of the Mystical

Understanding the prophetic language of God is not a formula—it's a relationship. I know I've said that already, but it's so important to grasp this truth in our pursuit of revelation. Friendship with God is the key to revelation secrets. We can be as close to the Lord as we choose to be. Jesus confides in His friends. Understanding this simple truth is powerful. Relationship with God unlocks revelation, as Jesus says He reveals to His friends what He hears from God:

> *I have never called you "servants," because a master doesn't confide in his servants, and servants don't always understand what the master is doing. But I call you my most intimate and cherished friends, for*

I reveal to you everything that I've heard from my Father (John 15:15 TPT).

RELATIONSHIP WITH GOD UNLOCKS REVELATION.

When we have a many-faceted encounter or experience in God that is beyond understanding in that moment, remind yourself that God unlocks the mystical for His friends. He promises, *"I instruct you in the way of wisdom and lead you along straight paths"* (Proverbs 4:11 NIV).

Supernaturally Normal

At the very start of the Bible, God said, *"Let there be light"* (Genesis 1:3) and began speaking the universe into existence. We want a supernatural God who reaches into our world and speaks, and yet sometimes we're shocked that He actually is supernatural! God's normal is supernatural, and as we emulate Him, hearing God's prophetic voice in our everyday life looks like being supernaturally normal.

At the very core of it, when God is interacting with us, He is delivering a message to us. The entire Bible is one long love letter to humanity from our heavenly Father. As God continues to speak into our world, it's not meant to be so complicated that we can't hear the heart of the Father. Whether we are reading the Bible and one of the verses jumps off the page with a message we need to hear, or something more out the box is happening, we can trust that God will reveal His heart to us. We can trust that God is not trying to confuse us or trip us up with intellectualism or unending mysticism. God is revealing a message through the mystical language of the encounter.

Remind your heart that a simple message is good. You don't have to come up with some long-winded message from an encounter you've had or a dream or sign that manifested. God may simply be saying, "I love you," or reminding you He's bigger than your circumstances, and that's enough. Sometimes the main message is the emotion you feel, like urgency to pray, or the tenderness of God toward you, renewed hope, or a fresh perspective toward a situation.

Often the first thing you sense God saying is actually what He's saying. There may be other details to discern, but "My sheep hear My voice" applies to hearing God through supernatural encounters.

My encouragement to you when you are working through what God is saying to you from an encounter is "Don't over-complicate the message!"

Look for the Main Theme and Don't Miss the Forest for the Trees

"Some people can't see the forest for the trees" is a saying that describes how some try and understand God's prophetic voice (I write this while smiling). In our eagerness to take it all in, we can miss the obvious because we get so bogged down with every little detail; somehow the main meaning of what God was saying is missed. It's not that details aren't impor-tant, as they often are. It's not that deeper revelation is not being released, as it often is. It's just that the little details can often trip us up and prevent us from focusing on the overall message that is often front and center. Getting stuck on the small details can prevent you from seeing past the mystical imagery to the main message.

When contemplating a dream, vision, or prophetic sign or encounter, ask yourself, *What is the main theme? What is the most important point? Is there something I immediately know God is saying? What is my immediate emotional response to this?*

Worship in the Midst of Mystery

Ultimately, God is purposefully getting our attention with any supernatural interaction with us. Even if you're unsure of the meaning, you can know that God is trying to get your attention. So you can stop and pray and ask for wisdom. You can also thank God for getting your attention and take it as an opportunity to worship God in the midst of the mystery of not yet fully understanding what He is saying.

That's a big key to relationship with Him. Worship Him in the midst of mystery, while you wait to understand the message. Stay engaged in the process of searching out a matter, but worship in the midst of mystery. The temptation is to allow frustration to disconnect us from pursuit of the Message Giver if the message requires some searching out. Instead of being frustrated, worship in the midst of the mystery.

Take "the unexplained yet" as a signpost to worship and be thankful until further revelation comes. Hope in the process of seeking revelation is always our own responsibility to steward.

Building Faith for More

God not only loves you, but He's also invested in you. He believes in you and is purposefully leading you, imparting to you, equipping you, and showing you how much He loves you through every interaction with Him, including the unusual, creative and even out-of-the-box encounters.

But why would God speak in prophetic symbolism and supernatural signs? Simply, because it builds faith in us for more. God speaks prophetically. And He loves to speak in whatever way necessary to ensure we receive His message. God understands that our minds can perceive something; but when our heart connects as well, we've truly got it.

For example, when a friend tells us a story, we understand in part; but if they show us photo of what they are talking about, we have a deeper connection with the story. I can tell you about an incredible meal I've had, or I can show you a photo. Better still, what if I could access some matrix-like, dream-inducing, real-time experience for you to actually taste my meal! You'd understand with the same sense of, "Oh wow, that's heaven on a plate!" that I felt about it.

God is the Master Communicator. He knows how to deliver a message that will mark you for the rest of your life, and get His point across brilliantly. God accesses your spirit and downloads encounters that speak a message to only you. He can give you instant impartation, new revelation, insight beyond natural observations, and compassionate upgrades. The mystical, supernatural nature of the King's prophetic voice is as important as the message itself sometimes. He's stirring your faith in the supernatural.

Your Personal Story and Language with God Unlocks the Mystical

The prophetic voice of the King is indeed very personal and purposeful. And He's very good at getting His message across to you in ways that will mark and define you.

Understanding His voice and ways will never make sense outside of relationship with Him. As we spend time with God and learn how His voice sounds to us, we build our personal and unique story with Him.

How God speaks to me is likely different from how God speaks to you. There will be similarities, but honestly, friendship is a personal thing. Heart connection is everything. The closer the friend, the more "inside" language you have. It's the same with God. The mystical imagery God uses to convey a message to me may mean something different to you.

My husband, Ben, and I can simply look at each other and know what the other is thinking. Sometimes I'll say just one word, and we laugh as it reminds us of a whole conversation we've previously had, or an "inside" joke, and we laugh all over again. Through forging friendship, we have built our own heart language, our own unique story with each other—shared memories and family traditions and funny moments.

For instance, I know that Ben loves noodles, and *Kung Fu Panda* is one of his most favorite movies (yes, it really is; that and *Madagascar 2!*). So if he asked me what I wanted for dinner and I sent him a gif of Kung Fu Panda on a mountaintop, he would immediately know I wanted noodles. And in a similar way, many of our conversations become lines from a favorite movie that Ben will say to me.

It's similar with God. As friendship grows, our personal story grows through history shared, time in prayer, and conversation; and over time, a personal language develops between you and God. He knows you! He wants you to know Him. And He loves speaking to you in ways that only your very best Friend can.

I encourage you to take note of the personal prophetic language between you and God. For instance, God speaks to me through pineapples. Yes, really!

A pineapple is obviously a fruit and can represent hospitality, but to Ben and me (and many others now) it now represents revival. We hosted a revival on the Sunshine Coast of Australia for around 18 months, and it was held in a building called the Big Pineapple. It's well known to tourists for the 50-foot pineapple looming in front of the building. Because of this, the revival became known as "The Pineapple Revival." In fact, we now call the humble pineapple the International Symbol of Revival!

Since then I've had dreams with pineapples, received every kind of pineapple gift you can imagine, and God has used the prophetic symbol of a pineapple at different moments to grab my attention and stir faith in me for breakthrough and revival. I've even had an encounter in a meeting where many smelled the fragrance of pineapple juice. It's been one of the more fun ways God has talked to me.

My point here is that pineapples came to mean something to me, and God uses them to stir faith in me. They are part of my personal language with Him, and symbolize revival to me.

The caution is this. It's about friendship, not formula. Just because a pineapple most often represents revival to me doesn't mean it's a formula that is set in stone. The key is friendship with the Message Giver.

> MYSTERY BECOMES A MESSAGE WHEN
> WE DEVELOP OUR STORY WITH GOD.

Mystery becomes a message when we know our God and build our own personal connection and story with Him. Look for the language of the Spirit that is part of your story with the Lord. Are there certain phrases or symbols that are unique to God's language with you?

God's Mystical Purpose is to Capture Your Heart

God isn't a textbook or a formula to follow. The purpose of the written Word of God—the Bible—is to lead us to *"The Word became flesh..."* (John 1:14 NIV). The prophetic voice of the King, the supernatural nature of His interactions with us, the mystical encounters and dreams all remind us that knowing God and His ways requires more than studying proven keys and formulas. Accessing God's revelation requires pursuing personal, authentic friendship with the King. God has always been after our heart. The foundation for understanding the mystical is building intimate connection with God over time.

In my early 20s I had an encounter that marked me with the truth that God is after my heart. I was heartbroken at the time. All the plans I had made for my life, and put my trust in, came crashing down. I was suddenly without income or a home, and I was tortured by the thought that my future was ruined. If you've ever been there, you know what I mean. At the time, I felt unloved, alone, broken, and scared of life; I struggled to see a way forward.

I found myself at my nana's house, a safe place to hide from life in that moment. As I cried myself to sleep one afternoon, I had a very *real* dream.

In the dream, I was sitting on a hill looking out over the most beautiful and glorious countryside. The grass was greener than I'd ever seen. As far as my eye could see were colorful flowers. The ones closest to me were a vibrant orange, and yet that is a poor description of something heavenly as they emanated otherworldly color and glory. As the wind blew, the flowers gently swayed and bent in unison like a ballet company dancing. That might sound strange, but the whole scene was alive and comforting. The air smelled sweet; and as I breathed it in, I was refreshed. Each breath took the weight of the world off me, and I was filled with tangible hope. I was surprised by an excitement for my future, and I realized the sadness, which had plagued me, was completely gone.

As I sat and stared at this peaceful place, a man walked toward me and sat down beside me. Instantly I knew He was Jesus. He exuded love, but more than that, completeness. The way He just walked over and quietly sat with me brings me to tears even now. I was aware He knew the disappointments and hurts. He saw all my fears. Not a word was said out loud, and yet a conversation took place that somehow spoke to my every broken place and concern. I had never felt so loved. As we sat there, I felt heard and fully seen. Love was a Person, and He was sitting next to me on a hill.

We sat on a hill together for what seemed an eternity until all I needed to hear was heard in my spirit. We laughed, we talked, we spoke of days to come. I don't remember the conversation now, but I know I'm living the days we talked of even then.

Then my eye was drawn again to the vivid, glorious orange flowers that resonated life and lived to worship God. I don't have words for some of the beauty and colors I saw. As we looked out over the valley and hills, I just knew He was writing on my heart, "Everything will be okay, Jodie." Somehow I knew Jesus was saying, "There are valleys and hills ahead, but I will never leave you."

I was sitting with the King—King Jesus. And yet in that moment, He was my Friend. The King was my Friend.

Then Jesus reached out in front of me and picked one of the flowers from the field. I remember being aware of the significance of the gift. This flower didn't wither or die, nor did His love for me. As Jesus handed me the heavenly flower, His eyes spoke a thousand whispers of His joy in me. He held out the flower to me and simply said, "For you because I love you."

Then I woke up.

As I awoke, I thought it was real. I could feel the stem of the flower in my hands. Reality was kicking in that I had only been dreaming, and I was sad it was just a dream, but I felt different. Dream or real, something was etched in my heart that was real. I smiled and thought, *Jesus gave me a flower.*

Suddenly there was a knock at my nana's front door. I jumped up, went to the door, and was surprised to see a dear childhood friend I'd not seen in quite some time. She was holding a bunch of bright orange flowers that looked strangely like the ones in my dream.

As I looked at them, tears were welling up in my eyes as she handed me a card. I remember it still. It was white with a simple teddy bear on the front holding a single orange flower. Then I noticed the words embossed on the card under the flower, "For you because I love you."

Now I really cried. Whether I was somehow in Heaven or dreamed of Heaven doesn't matter. Jesus visited me and told me He loved me. I still see those words etched in my heart sometimes, "For you because I love you."

Let me emphasize something: I *knew* God loved me. But after that encounter, I *felt* loved by God. I've never forgotten that encounter. Still to this day when I see bright flowers or see an orange flower, I remember Jesus saying, "For you because I love you."

Mentoring Moment with the King

- What are some examples of the "personal language of the spirit" that you and the Lord have?
- Are there phrases or ways God speaks to you that means something just to you?
- Have there been times you've overcomplicated what God is trying to say to you?

- When evaluating your encounters that are more mystical, look for the purpose. Describe a time when God has shown you His purposes in the midst of challenge that encouraged you. How did He do that?

- Have you ever had an encounter that was "heavenly"? How has that influenced you?

- The journey from mystical to message provokes faith in God's supernatural power. How is your faith being provoked right now?

- Remind yourself that God loves you. Think of an encounter or experience where you felt or knew His love. How did that impact your connection to God?

- Is there an encounter that is more mystery than message right now to you? Worship God in the midst of mystery.

- Thank God for His loving voice that will lead you into increasing wisdom.

Activation Prayer

Holy Spirit, would You expand my capacity to experience Your voice in my life and stretch my heart to receive Your love in deeper ways. I want to see beyond the mystical to the message of Your joy in me. Expand my heart to receive from You. I love how You love me so well, God. Amen.

3

UNLOCKING THE VEILED AND HIDDEN

O<small>NE OF THE DEFINING VALUES OF</small> J<small>ESUS'</small> <small>MINISTRY ON</small>
earth was that He reached into the hearts of every-
day people; He constantly reminded people that serving God
was about authentic relationship. God looks at the heart; and
in this regard, childlike hunger rates higher in the Kingdom
than jostling for supposed position and power. Over and over
Jesus made it clear that that *"Blessed are those who hunger and
thirst..."* (Matthew 5:6 NKJV).

Matthew 11:25 (TPT) says, *"...And you have hidden the
great revelation of your authority from those who are proud and
think they are wise and unveiled it instead to little children."*

THE KEY THAT UNLOCKS AND UNVEILS REVELATION IS CHILDLIKE HUNGER.

Put simply, spiritual understanding and revelation is
unlocked by childlike hunger. There are some things in the

Kingdom that are only accessed via hunger to seek, including discerning the King's prophetic voice. If we want to access Kingdom revelation, we need to learn, or re-learn, how to be like little children—trusting, pure in motive, and have child-like faith to receive. The Bible even goes so far as to say that there are things hidden from the proud and those who think they are wise. This implies there are some glory realm encounters and prophetic symbolism revealed through mystery that will only be unveiled through *hunger*.

The discipline of growing in skill, wisdom, and knowledge are worthy pursuits. However, Jesus highlights that some spiritual truths are not found through intellectual pursuit alone, but through raw faith and hunger. The truth is there are hidden and unveiled things to discover in the Kingdom. Childlike hunger after God will give you access to places that spiritual pride will lock you out of. That's huge!

Spiritual pride hinders teachability and is a wet blanket to hunger. Let's look again at what Jesus says in Matthew 5:6 (NKJV), *"Blessed are those who hunger and thirst for righteousness for they shall be filled."* Jesus is saying that hunger is not only blessed, but answered! Hunger will open doors to blessing, that lack of hunger will not. As we hunger for God and His righteousness, we are filled with God and His righteousness.

What does this have to do with hearing the prophetic voice of God? *You*, my friend, have all that you need in the Holy Spirit to hear, recognize, and translate what God is saying to you. It takes a treasure hunt sometimes, but you're equipped through the Holy Spirit, and given access through your childlike hunger. The school of the spirit is open as He unveils the hidden things to your hungry heart.

Hunger Leads You to Jesus

Herod, as recorded in Matthew 1, is an interesting example of getting it all wrong. Herod was led by self-seeking power. The Magi, however, were led by hunger to find the prophesied Messiah and a supernatural sign—a bright star—led them. The same star was seen by others, but even Herod in all his positional power and wealth was unable to crack the code and understand the signs and prophetic messages around him that led to Jesus. Of course, King Herod had completely impure motives—and that's the point. All his power and knowledge could not unlock what the hunger and pure hearts of the Magi did as they came to worship Jesus.

It also reminds us that God speaks our language. The Magi had given a lifetime to studying scriptures and understanding prophetic signs in the stars and times. God spoke to them through their personality, their training, and used terms and prophetic language that they understood.

HUNGER FUELS THE TREASURE HUNT.

The symbolic nature of the prophetic voice of God can sometimes circumvent our reasoning to speak directly to our spirit. God is good at laying treasure hunts that lead to Jesus. The point is though, the treasure hunt is not the end goal, the treasure is—God. Hunger is the gas that fuels the treasure hunt.

Searching and Translating Symbolic Language

At a base level, the purpose of God's prophetic voice in our life is simply God messaging us something He wants us to translate and understand. He speaks in ways that get our attention. If it's repetitious, outside our normal, or symbolic, it interrupts our busy lives on purpose—because that's the point. It is intended to make you stop and ask, "Is this God?" and "What does this mean?" "What are You saying to me through this?" His prophetic voice is a treasure map, to point us to a deeper message, and ultimately to God.

Too often we are so consumed with the noise and busyness of life, that it's easy to focus on everything else except what really matters most in life—things of eternal value. When we hear God in a creative, prophetic way, God in His kindness is cutting through the noise and delivering a message to us. As finding the meaning requires some searching, it reminds us of the joy of discovery. Without hunger we will abandon the search.

Search Out and Translate a Matter

Proverbs 25:2 (NKJV) says, *"It is the glory of God to conceal a matter, but the glory of kings is to search out a matter."*

There's honor in searching for the treasure. God knows very well that when the search takes some effort, the thrill of discovery means so much more! The searching out a matter is the process of translating the King's prophetic voice. And the process of translating is intended to add glory in our lives. The glory of God is found in the hunger to search. The hungry shall be filled.

I've heard Pastor Bill Johnson say many times, "God doesn't hide things *from* us, but *for* us." Wisdom is grown when seeking God. There's a glory in searching out a matter with God. That literally means that great influence is upon those who will seek the Messenger for wisdom. And those who search, find. Hunger is Kingdom currency. Hunger causes you to seek for more of God. Hunger sets you apart in the Kingdom.

After a journey that takes some time and effort to "search out a matter," you're not likely to easily forget what you searched out and discovered. In searching out a matter, we are seeking the divine nature of God and building connection to God. As said earlier, the act of seeking righteousness finds what we're looking for, not just the message, but the Messenger. Importantly, translating God's prophetic voice will lead you to Jesus.

CULTIVATING HUNGER RECALIBRATES YOUR INNER COMPASS.

Cultivating hunger after God will recalibrate the compass of your heart and upgrade your ability to discern what God is saying through His prophetic and supernatural ways. It's one thing to hear God, but another to understand what He's saying.

Take moments every day and seek the Messenger Himself, for no other reason than to connect with God. Those who do this not only find God, but fine-tune the inner compass that hears directions and discerns revelation from the Lord.

Deciphering His Message

I'm an Australian currently living in the United States—Arizona to be exact. Yes, the desert landscape and heat is quite different from the tropical beaches of Queensland we left behind in Australia. Before Arizona, we called Texas home. For four years, we've lived in America, sent as missionaries to this great land. What a journey so far. Certainly, it's been amazing to see God's provision and timing. When we first heard God call us to America, we felt the urgency of the call. Specifically, we heard, "It's now or never!" Through many prophetic nudges, words, dreams, confirmations, and supernatural ways, the Lord spoke to us, "this is urgent." This was a *rhema* word to us, and it came with such an urgency that we packed up our lives and all that entailed very quickly and moved across nations from Australia to the United States. The unfolding past season in the nations has served to exemplify the wisdom of following the Lord's voice quickly when a message is urgent.

My Aussie Accent Stands Out

My Aussie accent makes my voice stand out in conversations with Americans because it's different. Depending on where I am in the country, my Aussie accent is hard for people to understand and I have to repeat myself before I'm fully understood. My accent itself stands out, gains attention, and often prompts people to ask questions. This happens even if I'm just ordering a hamburger or coffee. The same happens when I travel to other nations. My accent draws attention and sparks interest in those who hear it.

However, when I'm home in Australia, I just sound like everyone else. Nobody finds my ordering of a hamburger or coffee particularly interesting or unusual. My point? An accent in a foreign setting stands out and cuts through the noise of familiarity because it's different from what people are used to hearing. It prompts interest and starts conversations.

A supernatural encounter or experiencing God's prophetic voice is just another form of communication. It's like an accent if you will, a different-sounding language that cuts through the noise of life and captures your attention. When God speaks to you in an unusual or symbolic way, His prophetic voice will cut through the noise of your life in a way that you will take notice of and remember.

Supernatural Rain

Throughout our ministry, *supernatural rain* has been one of the most common prophetic signs I have experienced. When I feel the rain, it's always a sign to me of First King's 18:41 (NIV), *"...there is the sound of a heavy rain,"* which prophetically was speaking about drought-breaking rain. Revival is spiritual drought-breaking rain.

I have had seasons when I've felt supernatural rain—which feels exactly like rain falling on my skin, but I'm inside under a roof—every day, if not multiple times a day. Still to this day, if it starts raining outside, I will almost always feel rain falling in the spirit on my skin.

God has used rain as a prophetic call to decree revival in my life, along with the message of *"abundance of rain"* (1 Kings 18:41 NKJV), but God has also used feeling supernatural rain to catch my attention to decree healing for someone. For instance, many times when I've ministered online, I have felt rain drop on a particular part of my body, and God has shown me it's a word of knowledge for someone's healing. If I'm praying for somebody and I start to feel rain, I always know God is refreshing and reviving that person. Supernatural rain has truly become a common sign in our lives of revival and God breaking in.

Now I only have to feel the tiniest drop of supernatural rain and I'm immediately praying for revival and pressing in for breakthrough. It's a fast track to an entire download of a message that births action.

I am convinced that our hunger for revival—which is Jesus, as we have decreed for the past twenty years, "I hear a sound of heavy rain" and interceded for God to "pour it out"—has in part, unlocked this supernatural rain encounter in our lives. Hunger is currency in the Kingdom.

Strongholds of Faith

Common ways God speaks to us, or past encounters, become fast tracks into breakthrough for us. When God's prophetic voice breaks into our lives and releases breakthrough or anointing to us, we can access that same breakthrough anointing by revisiting the encounter. It becomes what I call, a stronghold of faith. You can revisit a past breakthrough you received again and again. In this way, you grow in authority to carry and release this to others. This is the kind of strongholds I want in my life—strongholds of faith, birthed from the King's prophetic voice in our lives.

What is a fast track into God's presence for you? As I mentioned, supernatural rain immediately stirs love for Jesus and passion for revival in me. Equally, reading favorite Bible passages such as Ezekiel 37 will do the same. What is a way God speaks to you that opens up a bigger message and points you to His heart? Think of a past dream or encounter that opened up a realm of faith for you, and revisit this by reminding yourself what God showed you, taught you, and imparted to you.

God Whets Our Appetite

The content of this book has been formulated over many years as the result of the supernatural encounters I've experienced and my wrestling to discern His voice and then explain what God was saying in biblical language.

Many of the signs and wonders I've experienced were unusual when they first happened, but they encouraged me to seek answers and grow in my faith and hunger for the impossible. I am grateful God has spoken to me in creative, supernatural ways, as it shows me God's personality, as well as His power. I've needed that in my journey. I know I wouldn't be doing what I'm doing today if it were not for God constantly showing me how powerful He is.

> *The Spirit of God whets our appetite by giving us a taste of what's ahead. He puts a little of heaven in our hearts so that we'll never settle for less* (2 Corinthians 5:5 *The Message*).

In other words, He makes us hungry for Him! And our hunger unlocks even more of the veiled and the hidden things of His Kingdom. It then becomes our responsibility to steward our hunger.

Over the years when I've hungered for more of God, I have experienced the miraculous. For example, an angel stood on the end of our bed, the same number sequence repetitively chased me down, gold leaves manifested in front of me, Jesus appeared in my dreams, diamonds dropped in front of me, and I received many visions that spoke of others who needed a touch from God. Many encounters have happened that made me wonder, and realize that God is bigger than my stuff. He whets our appetite with His prophetic voice—and waits to see if we will seek Him for more.

Ask yourself what God has been doing in your life to whet your appetite for more. Have you taken the invitation to seek Him in that area? In what parts of your life can you see observable, increased faith?

The prophetic encounter is an invitation to more. It's intended to grow our hunger and faith for more. Ask yourself where God is inviting you to stretch your hunger, as hunger is a catalyst that unlocks revelation. .

Recognizing the Invitation to Receive More of Him

As we realize that God has been whetting our appetite to pursue Him for more, we recognize the invitation in the actual encounter. God has your attention, so let's accept His invitation to be like little children stirred to hunger. If our family and community are not benefiting from the King's prophetic voice in our lives, we must revisit what God has been saying and doing and actively pursue hunger and faith for more of Him.

May our prayer be something like this: "What You've done for me, Lord, You will do for others. What You've given me access to I will make a stronghold of faith that stewards and releases the same over others. You've whet my appetite and I say yes to all You're offering me."

Mentoring Moment with the King

- How has God whet your appetite for more?
- What encounters with the King's prophetic voice have given you an invitation to pursue more?
- How has God used encounters with the supernatural or His voice to stretch your faith?
- Consider where you have strongholds of faith as a result of how God has grown you.
- How has your family and sphere of influence benefited from the King's voice in your life?

Activation Prayer

Lord, reveal to me any encounters with You that were intended to spark hunger for the things of You that I can reactivate and pursue. I ask for insatiable, contagious hunger after Your heart, God. I invite You to provoke me to new levels of hunger. I love You, Lord, and I love how You speak to me. Amen.

4

TRANSLATING THE ENCOUNTER

Growing up, I had lots of supernatural experiences, most of which I didn't fully understand. The one thing I did always know was Jesus loved me, and I'm so thankful Jesus' love constantly intervened in my life and led me into greater wisdom.

Sadly, most of the encounters I had initially were dark and tried to grip my heart with fear. I knew even then that Jesus was more powerful, but I also knew there was a demonic realm, because I'd experienced it. I knew the intention of the demonic was to entrap me in fear, taint my understanding of God as a good Father, and stop my pursuit of His prophetic voice by making me too scared to interact with a supernatural God.

Many, many people I meet have had similar experiences growing up that have continued into their adult lives. It brought fear and torment that has tried to control them, prevent joy in their relationship with God, and shut down their prophetic, seer gifting.

Evicting Fear

I am aware now that this is a common experience for many. The good news is that rebuking, binding, and evicting the enemy in Jesus' name works! I have a fire in my belly now to break the chains of demonic fear that has tormented and shut down too many people for far too long called to release and experience the prophetic voice of God. It's not okay; it's not God's heart. King Jesus has given us authority to cut off fear and chains of darkness, and enjoy prophetic encounters in the glory realm. Evicting fear from your life allows you to experience fully your supernatural, loving God and translate what He is saying to you.

Of course, the intention of the enemy going after me and so many others is to make us scared of the prophetic, seer gift on their life. If the devil can make people afraid of the glory realm, they will shy away from supernatural encounters with God. Fear is not from God; fear is a spirit—but it is *not* the Holy Spirit, and fear must go in Jesus' name.

Do not allow the enemy to mold your expectations of what a relationship with your loving God looks like. I declare this over you right now: I speak a recalibration in your heart wherever the enemy has tried to convince you that your experience and relationship with a supernatural God and the King's prophetic voice is anything but life giving and faith building. I evict fear and torment from your life in Jesus' name. I especially evict fear of fear and torment in your pursuit of God and His supernatural ways. Fear of fear and torment if you fully activate your prophetic gift must leave in Jesus' name. Your connection to God is blessed, and the way you hear, see, and encounter the glory realm with King Jesus is blessed. You will live free from the torment of fear and be filled with peace. In Jesus' name, amen!

> *Submit yourselves, then, to God. Resist the devil, and he will flee from you* (James 4:7 NIV).
>
> *For God has not given us a spirit of fear, but of power and of love and of a sound mind* (2 Timothy 1:7 NKJV).

Read these verses over and over until they come alive in you. Decree over yourself: "Fear has no hold on me; fear will not impact my future days, my experience of God, or steal my fierce courage to run hard after God and enjoy connection with Him. I will grow and thrive from His prophetic voice in my life!"

If an encounter paralyzes you with fear, ungodly thoughts, lies, and is devoid of God's love, this is *not* an encounter from God. There's no need to be fearful of the enemy, but rather rebuke the devil and he will flee in Jesus' name. It's that simple. Tell fear to go in Jesus' name.

I am laboring on this important truth because so many people are more fearful of the dark, demonic realm than they are of *not* pursuing God. Fear must be evicted in our pursuit of God so we can fully walk in our call. Make the name of Jesus stronger within you than fear of the enemy. *"You are of God, little children, and have overcome them, because He* [Jesus] *who is in you is greater than he* [the enemy] *who is in the world"* (1 John 4:4 NKJV).

I have woken in the night at different times (rare now, but it has happened) and sensed a darkness or fear in my room. I've immediately known it was not God, but demonic. I'm only mentioning this because something similar has happened to many I pray with. I simply tell the fear and anything from the devil to go in Jesus' name. Remind yourself that Jesus is greater, Jesus is higher. God is for us, so who can be against us (see Romans 8:31). Speak the peace of God over yourself and your home in Jesus' name. I do that right now over you, "Peace in Jesus' name."

Insight for Breakthrough

Sometimes God gives us insight into the enemy's strategies for the purpose of winning the breakthrough. God gives us the upper hand through higher revelation to use in intercession and bring the breakthrough.

This happened in the Bible when God told Gideon to go and listen to what the enemy was saying the night before he was going to battle (Judges 7:13-25). God had given the enemy dreams that put the fear of God in them, and showed them Gideon would win. It was all prophetic language, mind you, but even the enemy was able to interpret the dreams and know God was with the mighty warrior Gideon and God's people. The dreams put confusion and a holy fear of God into the enemy camp, giving victory in the battle to Gideon's army.

Obeying God and eavesdropping gave Gideon insight into what the enemy was thinking. God will do this for us too through prophetic encounters. Take note when He does, and use the insight in intercession for breakthrough.

The Enemy Is Scrawny

One morning I awoke to a vision and immediately knew I was seeing something demonic. I felt peace and knew God was allowing me to see for the sake of insight and intercession. What I saw was a vision of a scrawny, weak, small demon trying to open my prayer journal and read it, but it couldn't actually open it. I immediately rebuked it in Jesus' name and it left. I knew God was allowing me to see this, as week after week we were taking ground in the spirit in our church in Australia as we decreed revival. I understood from the encounter that the enemy was getting nervous as he was losing ground.

God also showed me that the enemy wanted to know what our plans with the Lord were so he could try and prevent them. But God guarded us, and the enemy couldn't see or interfere with God's plans. The enemy lacked anointed revelation and vision as this comes from God. The enemy wanted to know how to stop God's plans, but God was showing me *the scrawny devil* couldn't even open my journal to see my prayers and planning with God. It was symbolic of God saying the devil is on the run and wants you to think he will stop you, but I have superior intelligence and strategy than the enemy so keep pressing in for My strategies. I knew God was reminding me to keep asking the Lord for wisdom to move forward. God was giving us the strategy of decreeing Psalm 91:1 (NIV), *"Whoever dwells in the shelter of the Most High will rest in the shadow of the Almighty."*

We were able to turn God's prophetic voice from the vision into prayer and decree that the enemy would be thrown into confusion and his plans fail. We prayed that the plans of the

Lord would succeed and the enemy be defeated and scattered. God's people would arise in courage and come out from fear.

When God gives you insight into the enemy's camp, use it to pray with divine insight and see the enemy scattered. More often, God will birth hunger in you from such encounters to go after what you are called to do. For instance, if the enemy is trying to intimidate you, you know God is adding courage to you, and the enemy is scared of your new authority. Ask for courage all the more!

GOD USES SIGNS TO DIRECT US.

In my journey, I've experienced many different signs and wonders. Some I talk about, some I hold close to my heart. All of them have pointed to Jesus and amplified God's power and love in my life.

God has used these encounters and His prophetic voice as signposts in my life, just like road signs that point the way when driving a vehicle.

All signs direct us, and signs from God always direct us or point us to Jesus. It they don't—don't follow them! But if they do point to Jesus and confirm His word, then of course we should take notice. Signs are never the problem, it's where they point us to that is the issue. God uses signs to point us to truth, and to nudge us in the direction He wants us to go.

Imagine if the wise men, the Magi, had not paid attention to the supernatural sign of the star that God used to lead them to the birth of the Messiah. God had no problem using His creation to give a prophetic sign that pointed straight to Jesus.

I don't even want to imagine if they had ignored that sign, and not translated what God was saying to them.

Rain with a Revival Message

As mentioned previously, supernatural rain has been a common manifestation of the supernatural that God has used in my personal life and our ministry. God has added so much joy and insight to me through this miraculous manifestation.

I remember well the first time I felt supernatural rain. My spirit leapt! I actually jumped up and down with excitement like a kid. Interestingly, I immediately knew it was God, and God was speaking through this strange phenomenon. I'd been sitting in my living room in Queensland, Australia, praying for revival, when suddenly it was raining inside my house! To be fair, there was no physical water, but I could feel the distinct sensation of rain falling on my skin. The more I decreed and prayed for revival, the heavier the rain became. Every drop infused me with radical faith and childlike joy.

My husband had also recently been feeling supernatural rain, and I love that God took us on this journey at the same time! Since then we have often experienced it in our lives and ministry. I feel rain start to fall as I press in and worship God or decree revival. Every time faith arises and to this day—I feel like a little kid joyfully jumping in puddles of rain.

Also mentioned previously, the message of the rain comes from First Kings 18, where the prophet Elijah was praying for drought-breaking rain. As he prayed, he heard the sound of heavy rain, which is incredible because there was a drought in the land with no sign of rain or clouds in the sky. In other words, rain was not forecast.

This one message became a call to contend for nation-shaking revival because Elijah heard the sound of heavy rain *before* there were even clouds. In a similar way you can hear the sound of revival about to break before it is manifest in the natural. After praying seven times, Elijah saw a "small cloud" on the horizon and knew the heavy rain would break the drought. Elijah heard the sound in his spirit of a new season, and this gave him faith to decree it into the now.

SUPERNATURAL RAIN PROPHESIES REVIVAL

When I felt the supernatural rain that day, it did the same! Spiritual, drought-breaking revival had not broken out over Australia yet, but I could hear its sound. I knew it had begun. I had faith for revival breaking out as we contended, because I could hear the sound of abundance of rain; in that moment, I could feel the rain falling on me! Revival may not have been forecast, but Heaven had a different forecast. Revival rain was coming to the nations!

We decreed this word all over Australia, from the outback to the cities. We decreed it all across the United States. We've decreed it all over the nations; and many times people in our meetings have felt supernatural rain as well. This one sign from God has imparted faith to shift the atmosphere from dry to hope again, and put a fire in our bellies to contend with "knowing faith" that Heaven is broadcasting revival rain on the horizon.

Physically when we feel rain, it's light like a sun shower, or heavy like a summer storm. But spiritually it always points to faith for revival breakthrough. My husband and I both feel supernatural rain at home sometimes as we pray. I've felt it the last few days writing this. It's become a personal kiss from God for us.

It always is a sign to me that there's more to come. God will pour out His presence and power in the nations. I hear a sound of heavy rain that may not be on the media's broadcast, but it's on Heaven's broadcast from the prophetic voice of the King. It's become a message that releases contagious faith for revival that's impartible, just at the whiff of rain in the air.

Is God showing you what Heaven is broadcasting over your family or nation? When God shows you what heaven is broadcasting, He is calling you to contend for this. God is giving you a strategy for intercession.

GOD GROWS US TO RECOGNIZE AND TRANSLATE THE NUANCES OF HIS VOICE.

As I've said before, what we steward grows. In fact, stewardship grows us to hear His prophetic voice more clearly.

There have been times when I smelled supernatural rain, just like it smells in the natural as rain starts to pour down. I can be ministering and all of a sudden I smell the fragrance of rain coming. It says immediately to me, "Press in, push a little further, the rain of refreshing and revival is about to break, don't stop now." Other times, I have seen the rain falling, or felt a few real raindrops with actual water manifesting in meetings while indoors—that's always amazing. When I feel the light rain, it often speaks to me of refreshing falling on God's people; when I feel the heavy rain, it often speaks to me of sudden downpour of breakthrough.

God has been growing in us an awareness not just of His rain but of the different types of rain, or even a sense of hard, dry ground that requires pounding to break up the soil so it is ready to receive. Recognizing these nuances, or ways He has spoken to us, didn't happen overnight, but have grown over seasons of persevering and staying faithful in the small things—the small clouds. God will do the same with you. Whatever and however God is talking to you, stay faithful in the small clouds and the heavy rain will come.

During times of seeking God and honoring God's prophetic voice, stay attuned to God as He speaks, as this grows our awareness of what and how He is speaking. As we steward our encounters, we grow in recognizing the nuances of His prophetic voice.

My husband and I have experienced supernatural rain in many different forms including thunder and lightning heard or seen by people during corporate worship. I've seen supernatural lightning drop as I've prayed and deliverance came. I've watched supernatural rain fall on crowds and unbelief is evicted. Often the rain has brought physical healing in my life. I've seen it do the same to other people. I want to be clear, Jesus is the healer, not the rain! But God uses signs, like rain, to point us to Jesus and activate our faith.

As an aside, faith is contagious. What you grow an authority of faith in, you can release to others. It's not about the rain, it's about Jesus. My point is—God's prophetic voice grows our faith in Jesus.

> ## GOD'S PROPHETIC VOICE GROWS OUR FAITH IN JESUS.

Diamonds with a Message

Similarly, yet in a more unusual way, God spoke to me at the start of the affectionately termed Pineapple Revival that my husband and I led and hosted, through diamonds.

God's presence was tangible and the atmosphere was electric. People were coming from near and far and there were incredible miracles. Healings were happening with ease, whole families were touched by God, including older kids who hadn't been in church for many years. Youth were walking in and getting saved publicly on the microphone and crying, "This is real, this is real!" and then their friends were saved too. Young children were having encounters with Jesus under the power of God for hours, including our own teenage daughter.

One time we heard a commotion suddenly erupting from various places in the building. We had been taking an offering and suddenly excited shouts were everywhere; we couldn't ignore what was going on. Then I heard someone say, "Wow, wow, it's a diamond!" People started running toward the front of the building to show us. Five different sets of people, from five different areas of the room all at once said that a diamond suddenly just *dropped* and appeared in front of them. The atmosphere was crisp and clean, I remember noting. Praise and victory shouts broke out, and a lot of "Wow God" could be heard. God was reminding us, "I'm the God of the impossible."

Ben and I already knew we needed to extend the revival because people were having life-changing, powerful encounters of salvation and destiny-transforming moments with God. Revival was in our midst. I wish I could open a window as I write and allow you to feel the tangible, electric, thick presence of God in the room that day. It was palpable. Overwhelming. Glorious. Faith building.

Interestingly, the number 5 in the Scriptures often has a biblical meaning of "grace and favor." I knew that. We were aware it was a sign. Five diamonds dropping in the offering on the last night of the revival when we were deciding to extend was a promise, a sign to those who were there—but it was also the very personal sign of grace and favor from the prophetic voice of the King to us.

My point? They weren't just diamonds to us. They weren't just amazing manifestations and a cool sign and wonder. They were kisses from Heaven with a prophetic message that was building our faith as we stepped out on the water with God. They were signs that built our faith to trust God for more. They were invitations to believe that the Giver of the message had more to pour out as we gave Him space.

The Pineapple Revival kept going night after night, week after week—18 more months since the "diamond offering" took place. Countless lives were saved, healed, and emboldened by God's revival presence. Jesus is the God of *all things are possible* (Matthew 19:26). We will never be the same. I don't want to be.

What is God adding to you from the encounters and signs He has brought into your life?

Mentoring Moment with the King

To steward the King's prophetic voice, write and record your encounters. Record the wisdom God gives you. Remember that revelation is an ongoing journey, so revisit what God has shown you from time to time as further wisdom comes. Take a moment and bless your relationship with God, and thank God He speaks.

These practical questions will help you translate and understand signs and encounters. They are designed to prompt your thinking processes, and stir fresh faith as you review your prophetic interactions with God and search out what God is adding to you. If you don't know an answer, just move on to the next question.

1. Does your encounter mean anything to you right away? Is there an obvious message?

2. Is there a Bible verse, truth, or faith story that the encounter is talking about or reminds you of?

3. Does the symbolism used mean something to you personally?

4. Does the symbolism used mean something to you after you research it?

5. Does it remind you of other encounters you have had or previous prophetic words?

6. In what way is He stretching your faith?

7. Is God showing you what Heaven is broadcasting over your circumstances, as opposed to what the enemy is broadcasting?

8. What is God calling you to believe and pray for?

9. What is He calling you to contend for?

10. What have you been praying about lately?

11. Is God giving you wisdom and strategy through this encounter?

12. What emotions does it stir in you?

13. Are there intercession strategies you can apply?

14. Is this encounter provoking hunger in you, and how can you steward that hunger?

15. How can you implement practical processes in your life and connection to God that will continue to steward the message of your encounter?

16. Ask God for wisdom where you don't understand yet. Give your questions to God and thank Him for wisdom.

17. Worship God in the waiting for further wisdom. Take a moment now and just tell Him what He means to you.

18. God is always building heart connection with you. How is God reminding you through the encounter that you are seen, loved, and that He is with you?

19. Tell God what He means to you and thank Him for what His prophetic voice is adding to your heart connection to Him.

Activation Prayer

Holy Spirit, I thank You for always building connection with my heart and pursuing personal friendship. Help me to contend for all You are prompting me to believe for. Lord, thank You for increased faith, and faith that believes beyond the limit of my comfort. I thank You for faith that believes for more than I have seen yet. I love You, even in the waiting and transitions of life, and I choose to see Your invitation in the encounter into greater intimacy and faith. Amen.

5

FOUNDATIONS TO HEARING GOD THAT ACTUALLY WORK

To know God's prophetic voice, we must know His still, small voice, and so fine-tuning the foundations of hearing God will increase our capacity to discern prophetic revelation.

Growing in hearing the voice of God in general is a topic for a whole other book in itself, but the same principles for hearing His still small voice are applicable to hearing God speak though supernatural encounters, prophetic symbolism, and signs and wonders. Some consider the foundations boring, and yet these keys unlock new revelatory realms of hearing the King's prophetic voice in your life.

Every way God speaks is God speaking! Did you get that? Whether God is speaking through the Bible, an inner voice to your heart, a dream, encounter, or angel waking you up in the night, it's all God! It's all His prophetic voice.

To know God's prophetic voice, we
need to know His still, small voice.

Hearing God for yourself is a crucial skill to refine and grow. The whole world is looking for something to hold on to that is secure, and God's word never changes even if circumstances do. God has given us access to His voice! That's not a small thing to be taken lightly. Defining our foundations helps us build strong connection to God for the seasons ahead.

Whoever Loves Jesus, Loves His Word

God speaks through the Bible. It would be wrong to minimize His Word, the Bible, as the foundation for hearing God. The Bible is the immutable, holy Word of God, and the foundation for discerning and judging all truth. If we say we love Jesus, we will make reading His Word a priority in our life.

Let's agree that when I refer to the prophetic voice of God, I am always placing the Bible as the preeminent source of truth.

Reading the Word of God and being filled with His Holy Spirit is the single most productive way to grow in hearing God and discerning His voice. Find ways to implement reading the Bible into your normal, everyday life; it builds you up and strengthens your faith. Reading the Bible is never wasted time.

The Bible is alive and active. Grab hold of this truth—it's mind-blowing. When I really caught that revelation, I understood that reading the Word would literally bring supernatural and natural change to me, and it made me extra passionate about reading it.

The Bible Is Alive and Active

For the word of God is alive and active... (Hebrews 4:12 NIV).

The Bible is literally like no other book. Unlike other books, the Bible is *alive and active*. When you read the Word of God, it actively works in you to bring about alignment to Kingdom truth. Because it's alive and living, it's transforming you from the inside to receive God's promises—things will literally change for the better from reading it.

> THE WORD OF GOD WORKS, BUT SOMETIMES YOU HAVE TO WORK THE WORD.

Books can inspire, but the Word of God carries power in and of itself to transform—as it is active and alive— as you meditate on it, soak in it, speak it out, read it. I think of the Word of God as "divine road workers" sent out to actively rebuild and work in our lives. As I say often, the Word of God works, but sometimes you have to put the Word of God to work!

I hope I'm instilling in you a love for the Word of God. The Bible is not a boring or a lesser way God speaks today. The Bible is the prophetic, powerful, supernatural voice of God in written form. As you read it though, it should birth a hunger to know the Author more, and personally experience the Jesus we are reading about in our lives. Scripture also grows discernment and wisdom.

For the word of God is alive and active. Sharper than any double-edged sword, it penetrates even to dividing soul and spirit, joints and marrow; it judges the thoughts and attitudes of the heart (Hebrews 4:12 NIV).

Strength in the Prophetic Comes From Relationship with the Holy Spirit

Hang with me, prophetic friend. I love prophetic people. I love the prophetic. I love encounters. I love God's prophetic voice. I love the supernatural and glory realm. I love all the ways God speaks to His people. I also know that the strength of prophetic people is relationship with Holy Spirit. The foundations of relationship with God are the Word and prayer, which only *add* to the encounters we experience. Actively building our foundations with God is the key to increased prophetic encounters.

So how do we build the foundations of our relationship with God? I think most of us would say we know how, which may be true; but the question is not do we know how, but do we actually do it?

A Blessing Prayer

I know your personal time with God is warred against by the enemy, so the following is a prayer for you as you determine to build your relationship with God through practical keys.

Dear friend, I bless your prayer life and your love of God's Word. I bless your time management and calendar. I bless your time with the Lord and say your heart will leap even now just thinking about His love for you and all the revelation He wants to pour out on you. I bless your thoughts as you think about your time with God, that you would come alive with joy and expectation of all God will add to your heart and entire life. I bless you to rise and shine as you meet with the Lord, your best Friend. I bless your friendship with God and your conversations and encounters with Him that revive and fuel your heart. I bless you in Jesus' name.

So with blessing upon you, let's look at some practical keys that unlock hearing God's prophetic voice.

THE BASICS ADD TO YOUR ABILITY TO INTERPRET PROPHETIC ENCOUNTERS.

Whether you've been hearing God your entire life or you're new to this aspect of your spiritual life, there's always more. These practical keys will help you hear God with greater clarity and discern what He's saying through the supernatural in your life.

The most common way people hear God is through His "still small voice" direct to our spirit, which is often described as thoughts that spring up from within our heart and resonate with peace.

Practical Foundational Keys to Hearing God

I encourage you as you read the next portion to let God highlight anything He is stirring in you to focus on or refine.

1. *Be still and create space.*

Psalm 46:10 (NKJV) says, *"Be still, and know that I am God."*

With all the everyday distractions, it's hard to be aware of God's presence. But as you purposefully make space for God's presence, you will become aware of Him in your daily life. When you are aware of God's presence, you will also be more aware of God's voice. God's presence is present and interactive in our lives.

Purposefully make a space that is peaceful so you can quiet your thoughts to focus on God. This may be a quiet corner in your bedroom, a comfy chair in the sunshine, a favorite spot at the beach, or a coffee in hand at the cafe while you tune out the *stuff of life* and "be still" on purpose. One of the best ways to do this is worship. Put on your favorite worship music, and welcome His presence.

When you're in that space, simply pray and ask Holy Spirit to speak to you. Imagine a time with a friend in a cafe if it helps, but invite God to be with you and speak.

Mentoring Moment: Do you have a space that you regularly meet with God? Where are your favorite places to connect with God?

2. *Know that God speaks your language.*

John 10:27 (NKJV) says, *"My sheep hear My voice, and I know them, and they follow Me,"* so thank God that you hear Him, and that it's easy to hear His voice, just as sheep hear and recognize their shepherd, you hear and recognize God. Let that truth fill you with good expectations of time spent with God. Evict any pressure, perfectionism, or fear. Remind yourself God knows how to speak to your heart.

Mentoring Moment: If hearing from God has been challenging in the past, speak over yourself this decree: "Hearing God is easy. I am made to recognize my Father's voice."

3. *Silence all distractions.*

By silencing all distractions, I simply mean take the practical steps mentioned to still your own distracting thoughts, the voice of others, and whatever is weighing heavy or filling your mind. Set worries, concerns, and distractions aside. Also, silence the voice of the enemy. Especially if you are plagued with fears, distractions, confusion, and doubts as you try to pray.

You can silence distractions by praying a simple prayer such as the following:

> *In the name of Jesus I welcome You, Holy Spirit, to talk to me. I speak a shield of protection around my time with You and silence any influence or intrusion of the demonic realm. I repent of any sin and ask for forgiveness. I ask You, Lord, to create in me a clean heart, with clean filters to hear You with clarity. I bind up all confusion, fear, doubt, fogginess, heaviness, and unbelief, and I release faith, joy, peace, and a sound mind. I am expectant of hearing Your voice. My ears will hear from You, Holy Spirit, and I thank You for speaking to me. In Jesus' name. Amen.*

4. *Ask God to speak to you; record what you hear.*

You can ask God specific questions or simply wait to hear what He wants to say to you.

To get started, a good question to ask is simply, "What do You want to say to me, Jesus?" Or, "What are Your thoughts about me today, Holy Spirit?"

When I'm praying I often ask, "Do You have anything to say to me, Holy Spirit? Or, "What are Your thoughts about this issue?"

Remember, don't make it complicated. Usually I just take note of the first thing I hear. You may hear just one word. That's great! Or you may just have a sense of something, like an immediate peace or that God is with you. You may "see" something, or have an entire revelation drop on you.

Whatever you hear, see, feel, or sense God is saying to you, take note of that. This stewards hearing God's voice, and also helps you remember what He said.

A caution: Everything we hear must be weighed against the Word of God. If you hear or see something that is blatantly not biblical, immediately evict that thought in the name of Jesus and listen again. For example, if you ask God what He thinks of you, and you hear, "I hate you and nobody wants to be your friend," you can know for a fact that was not the voice of God you heard. God loves you always and forever (see Romans 8:39; Ephesians 2:4; 1 John 4:7). Only the accuser, your enemy would say that. So evict it and just move on. Sometimes we have had a lifetime of listening to lies like that, so it's normal to have times of recalibration to truth as we wait on God. If it's not from God's heart, flush it from your mind and move on.

Some of us have spent decades refining the art of listening to the voice of our TVs, social media, and unwise influences, and so it can take a while to make new habits of removing distractions and ignoring the lies the enemy has tried to tell us for years. In truth, this is an ongoing process for all believers.

DON'T QUIT EVEN IF IT TAKES AWHILE.

What if you hear nothing from God?

Don't stress! I often don't hear an immediate response to a specific question. Sometimes I ask God a question, and He answers with a different question for me to answer! Sometimes God talks about something that seems unrelated, but trust God. You're building relationship, not ticking off a list of questions answered. God always gives wisdom to those who ask. And time with God is never wasted.

> *If any of you lacks wisdom, you should ask God, who gives generously to all without finding fault, and it will be given to you* (James 1:5 NIV).

5. *Keep it simple and focus on Jesus.*

It's okay to be with someone you love and not talk sometimes. In fact, it's a sign that you are comfortable in each other's presence. It's the same with God. Be okay with just being in His presence and not always trying to hear something.

If you make this about friendship, you've already won! Just take the time to be with the Holy Spirit and enjoy His presence. You will recognize the nuances of His voice with greater clarity over time.

Remember, the more you steward time with God, the easier it is to recognize His voice and translate what He's saying to you in prophetic, supernatural ways.

Just focus on Jesus, and keep it simple.

Mentoring Moment: Ask yourself, *What does a tug at my heart from God feel like? How do I recognize when I'm "missing God," as in homesick for His presence? Are there telltale signs that tell me when I need to be with the Lord? How do I describe "the still small voice"?*

6. *Ask the Holy Spirit to lead you and enlighten the eyes of your heart.*

Prophetic encounters with God require supernatural revelation—and God reveals this to you when you ask Him. He enlightens the eyes of your heart.

Some of what you hear from God takes time to digest and interpret. That's okay. Hold it in your heart and give yourself time to process.

Revelation comes from the Holy Spirit, so pray that God would indeed enlighten the eyes of your heart, revealing wisdom and revelation of His glory realm to you.

> *I pray that the eyes of your heart may be enlightened in order that you may know the hope to which he has called you, the riches of his glorious inheritance in his holy people* (Ephesians 1:18 NIV).

Mentoring Moment

I've heard God in many unusual ways. Some I talk about, and some I hold close to my heart like Mary who *"treasured up all these things and pondered them in her heart"* (Luke 2:19 NIV). You can be assured though, friend, you don't need a degree of theology to know Jesus and grow in revelation, even for what you don't understand yet. Determine to prioritize friendship in practical ways. Are there prophetic encounters you've had that you are still pondering in your heart what God was talking about? Ask Him to reveal fresh revelation to you.

Holy Spirit Eye-Drops Dream

When I first heard someone speak on praying Ephesians 1:18 over ourselves, I prayed and asked God to open my eyes. That night I had a very simple dream of eye drops being administered to my eyes. Two drops were put in each eye. On waking, I was immediately aware that this was a sign that the Holy Spirit had indeed *enlightened the eyes of my heart* and brought increase. I also knew that there was still more! As we steward the small, increase comes.

Activation Prayer

Pray the following prayer for increased, supernatural enlightenment now:

Lord, enlighten the eyes of my understanding. I ask You for divine understanding to recognize Your voice in my life, and understand what You are saying to me. I ask for wisdom to recognize your prophetic voice and ways breaking into my life, and for You to lead me into wisdom. I ask for increase to see, hear, sense, and know Your voice in all the ways You desire to speak to me. I ask for increased visions, dreams, encounters, signs, wonders, and miracles. I ask for a stretching of my heart to receive as I seek You, Lord. I ask for encounters with You, God, that show me new aspects of Your holiness, glory, power, and love. Show me Your glory, Lord. Show me Your heart, Lord. Awaken my spirt to hear from You. Awaken every part of my being to Your realness and nearness. Open the eyes of my heart, Lord, to see You and know You more deeply. I love Your voice. I love You, Jesus. And I thank You for increased revelation, encounter, and knowledge from You. Amen.

Practical keys to hearing God summary:

1. Be still and create space.
2. Know God speaks your language.
3. Silence all distractions.
4. Ask God to speak to you; record what you hear.
5. Ask the Holy Spirit to lead you and enlighten the eyes of your heart.

Mentoring Moment with the King

Now, take a moment, grab a pen and paper…and wait on God.

Ask God to speak to you about an area of your life, or encounter you've had, or simply ask, "What would You like to say to me, God?" Then record what you hear or see.

I'm expectant for you, friend!

6

GOD'S PERSONALITY
IS CREATIVE

U NDERSTANDING THAT GOD CAN BE KNOWN, NOT AS A
book, but as a living God with a personality, transforms
and expands our expectations of how and what we hear from
Him. To translate the prophetic voice of God, we need to
understand He has a personality that we can get to know.

Of course God is holy and righteous, but He is equally
joyful and has a sense of humor at times. In fact, in His presence the Bible says there is, *"fullness of joy"* (Psalm 16:11
NKJV). And Romans 14:17 (NKJV) says, *"for the kingdom of
God is not eating and drinking, but righteousness and peace and
joy in the Holy Spirit,"* which tells us that joy is honored and
present in the Kingdom of God in the same way as peace
and righteousness.

It saddens me when I hear people talking about God without any emotional connection or joy, as this does not reflect
the God I know at all. It demonstrates lack of experiential

relationship with the God who actively talks to us, pursues relationship, and often interacts with us in creative ways.

The purpose of the Bible is to lead us to the God of the Bible. And surely the Bible shows us a God who loves passionately, protects connection fiercely, and desires family—not lifeless membership in an organization.

The first book of the Bible, Genesis, begins with the story of creation. Everything in our world that is beautiful and glorious came out of the heart and creativity of our God. The most stunning mountains you can imagine, your favorite beach, the desert landscapes, open plains and tropical wetlands—all of it came from the heart of God. After God created people—the pinnacle of creation— He called them "very good." He was pleased with His masterpiece.

There is so much glory in the creation Scriptures, but all I want to communicate to you is God didn't just create a world that is grey and dull and monotonous. Every landscape and creature is unique—not a copy of the last. The diversity of colors, the contrasts in nature, the multiplicity of vegetation, and the glorious intricacy and complexity of design in every living creature is infinitely glorious. The intelligence of design is a whole other conversation, but think for a moment about the creativity required for such a colossal masterpiece.

I can't watch a sunset without thinking of God our Creator personally painting the sky, with hues of orange and pink. Looking at the night sky or a snowcapped glacier, or a hidden beach with white sand and turquoise water, it's impossible to not feel small and recognize the enormity of our God the

Creator. Truly, He's exceptionally good at what He does—being a creator!

Our prophetic encounters with Him will also reflect the creativity of God. He is not boring, He is the Creator!

It's crazy to think that after Genesis God hung up His paintbrushes and told Himself to never have another creative idea, artistic thought, or innovative solution. God's creativity was not exhausted or depleted by creating the universe. His creative capacity remains available to tap into through the glory realm, and to experience through relationship with Him. It's astounding to me that we would ever expect our encounters with Him to be anything less than an alive, interactive, incredibly life-giving, engaging, experiential, innovative, and full of glorious beauty and anointed creativity.

The Thrill of Discovery

The thrill of discovery can never be underrated. Children live this reality as they daily discover new joys and master new skills, grasping concepts or achieving some small accomplishment that they celebrate with bubbling glee! Joy is intended to partner with discovery and learning, to teach us to seek out the manifold wisdom and glory of God. His glory realm extends from glory to glory, the unending majesty of the Lord.

In the process of discovering and developing relationship with your heavenly Father, you will quickly realize that God *oozes* creativity and will discover His creative personality can't be disconnected from His wisdom, or how He interacts with you.

God is not a dead or distant idol or a dry religion. We know this, and yet sometimes we still take issue when He exhibits too much color or creativity when He speaks. If we think an encounter is too expressive, supernatural, or emotive, it's good to remember that God is still the same God who created the universe. The King's prophetic voice is creative.

> IF YOU THINK GOD LACKS JOY OR CREATIVITY, YOU WILL STRUGGLE WITH MANY ENCOUNTERS, SIGNS, AND WONDERS THAT GOD SHOWS YOU TO GROW YOU.

I'm very much for preaching being "all in" and taking each season seriously. We must preach repentance, purity, and running our race at full speed. On the other hand, I also realize that God's prophetic voice reminds us that He most certainly is not one-dimensional or lacking joy and inspired creativity.

I Heard God Laugh All Night

Some years ago, I had a dream and heard God singing all night long the old spiritual song, "Dem bones, dem bones, dem dry bones, oh hear the word of the Lord!" Seriously, I felt like God sang this song all night to me! As I heard Heaven singing along, I could hear God laughing. Yes, I heard God laughing! A loud, belly laugh. It was contagious! It was hilarious. It was so funny, I found myself laughing along in my dream. I'm sure I was laughing in my sleep. Anointed joy broke out in my dream that I felt the next day. This encounter stretched my understanding of God's joy and His creative personality.

In the dream I saw an arid landscape and dry bones rising from the ground as God laughed. The whole scene was like an old-fashioned, slapstick, black and white comedy movie as freshly formed skeletons started dancing to the song, "Dem bones, dem bones, dem dry bones…," and God laughed all the more. As I watched I saw the numbers 1111 appear over the heads of the dancing skeletons and then the numbers 333 appeared floating over the skeletons as well.

Immediately, I knew that I was somehow watching Ezekiel 37 play out in front of me. I was seeing the end-time church arise that carried John 11:11 resurrection power to call forth Lazarus-style comebacks out of the grave. I also knew this church I saw rising carried an understanding of Jeremiah 33:3 to call to God and He will answer!

> *…Our friend Lazarus has fallen asleep; but I am going there to wake him up* (John 11:11 NIV).
>
> *Call to Me, and I will answer you, and show you great and mighty things, which you do not know* (Jeremiah 33:3 NKJV).

I was watching the dry bones arise *in* the joy of the Lord as God laughed and scoffed at His enemies. The end-time army will arise, marked by resurrection power, and be a house of prayer for the nations. This church is powerful! But what impacted me was not just the power to call forth dead things to life, but that God was so joyful—this was not hard for Him. I watched God laugh an army into existence. His joy was their strength (see Nehemiah 8:10b), literally, and Ezekiel 37 dry bones were prophesied to life *in my sleep*.

Hearing God laugh all night long was seriously contagious. It put such a joy in me. That wild dream marked me.

God sits in the heavens and laughs at His enemies! (See Psalm 2:4.) Revival will break out. An end-time prayer movement and *army* of God will arise. Ezekiel's bones will come to life. "Prophesy, son of man," Ezekiel's vision commands. Can a victorious church arise from dry and impossible circumstances in resurrection power? Yes! And the joy of the Lord will be their strength, literally! All this was communicated from a wildly creative dream from the King's prophetic voice.

I also know that God laughs. Have you had an encounter where the joy of the Lord surprised you with how real it was? Have you been amazed by the creativity of the Lord when He communicates?

Psalm 126:2 (TPT) says:

> *We laughed and laughed and overflowed with gladness. We were left shouting for joy and singing your praise. All the nations saw it and joined in, saying, "The Lord has done great miracles for them!"*

Jesus Cooked Me Dinner

One time I had an open-eye vision. I was awake and suddenly saw something drop in front of me. I walked into my kitchen and saw a well-known chef making dinner for me. I knew somehow this scene represented Jesus in my kitchen, and He wanted to show me something. As I watched the Chef, He had all my favorite ingredients out on the counter and was whipping up an incredible Italian feast from scratch that were all my favorites.

Suddenly Jesus was the chef, and He looked up at me with a warm smile and excitement in His eyes. Jesus was enjoying making me an Italian feast! He said, "I know you, Jodie. I know what you like and I know what makes you smile. It's my good pleasure to give you good gifts. I want you to enjoy what I'm serving you." Then, the vision ended.

I was dumbfounded. I had been struggling with enjoying God, or rather, enjoying blessing when God blessed me. I was okay with sacrifice, but not comfortable with enjoying God's goodness toward me. God was showing me that He enjoyed blessing me; and just as I would say thank you to a master chef if he showed up at my house to bless me, I should be thankful to God and value that He wants to do things that touch my heart.

Not only that, He's *very* creative! God enjoys creatively interacting with us. It's His joy to breathe life into the dry bones and weary dreams of our heart through His prophetic, creative voice.

Intense Seasons Require Extreme Joy

While the days are intense and talking about joy and laughter can at times seem trivial, in fact, during intense seasons of warfare, we need to understand the joy and creativity of the Lord more than ever. These two aspects of God's personality are literally our strength and will sustain us in this hour. His anointed creativity will bring the divine solutions we need.

God's voice will at times speak to us in ways that make us laugh or stretch our creativity, and give us hope, sometimes in unusual, creative ways. He always knows what we need when we need it. If we don't acknowledge God's creativity and joy, we may miss what He's saying to us.

Understanding God's prophetic voice through supernatural signs and symbolism requires having a grid for God's creative personality and value for joy. Otherwise you will reject at least one-third of what He is saying to you.

How do I know this? Righteousness, peace and joy. The Kingdom of God as defined by Romans 14:17 apportions one-third to joy! You'll choose to hear through righteousness, but reject joy and laughter. Or you'll hear Him though peace and holiness, but not Holy Spirit creativity that releases freedom.

> *For the kingdom of God is not a matter of rules about food and drink, but is in the realm of the Holy Spirit, filled with righteousness, peace, and joy* (Romans 14:17 TPT).

We need to hear our King through the fullness of who He is, the manifold wisdom and glory of God, or we miss much of what God is trying to give us through encounters with the King's prophetic voice.

DON'T GIVE THE DEVIL ALL THE CREATIVE LICENSE.

There is a demonic, deceptive dark realm, and I do not endorse dabbling in this or entertaining revelation that comes from a demonic source. We stay safe from that realm by being grounded in the Word, having an active relationship with God, and being connected to a Bible-believing, Spirit-filled power-manifesting community of believers. That should go without saying, but sometimes the things that should go without saying, need saying.

Sadly though, we often give the devil more right to be creative than we do the Holy Spirit!

Can I say that again? Some are okay with the devil doing supernatural things and accept the devil's ability to express dark creativity in how he influences and intimidates people—yet we squirm or worry if God speaks in a creative, joy-filled, supernatural way. We have to get past this misguided thinking. God is creative. God is joyful. So is His voice. And so will our encounters and interactions with Him be at times. The King's prophetic voice is gloriously creative and full of joy.

Mentoring Moment with the King

- Remind yourself of some of the most creative and fun ways God has spoken to you, and what He was imparting.
- Have you given the devil more creative license than God when it comes to speaking to you?
- Is God expanding your understanding of His personality to include more joy, fun, and creativity? Take a moment and ask if you have discarded some encounters based on limited thinking of who God is or a bias away from joy and creativity.

Activation Prayer

Holy Spirit, expand my revelation of Your creativity and joy. I ask for impartation of childlike joy, God, and for a new, creative flow in my connection to Your heart. Lord, would You help me embrace the fullness of who You are—holy, righteous, and joyful. I love the way You speak to me, Lord, and I receive Your glorious, anointed creativity flowing as I hear and experience You. Amen.

7

STEWARDING THE PROPHETIC VOICE OF GOD

STEWARDING WHAT THE LORD IS SAYING TO US INCREASES revelation in our lives and gives us the tools we need for breakthrough. It also increases encounters when we value His prophetic voice and steward what, and *how*, He says something. Stewarding what God gives us is a powerful Kingdom principle, and equally so when it comes to the King's prophetic voice. Without practical stewardship of the King's prophetic voice in your life, it's difficult to walk in the fullness of your call. God's mystical, prophetic voice must be actioned in practical ways.

Seeds grow. And stewardship of the small seeds in our life brings a harvest of multiplied more.

Action Is Required to Steward Something

Stewarding well the prophetic, signs and wonders, and whatever encounters you have, will also bring increase in your life. This increase will look different at different times depending on what God is saying and how you choose to steward it. But ultimately, action is required to steward the intent of what the Lord is saying to us. Even if the message is simply that He loves us—and this is never simple, it's profound—the stewardship of the message is applying its truth in the outworking of our daily lives.

Sometimes the stewardship of a dream, vision, or revelation that pertains to other people is passing on encouragement, a word, or praying for them. I am aware, however, that some people have dreams almost every night, and stewardship of this is not interpreting every last detail and spending all day every day to work out what you received in the night hours. We should look for the main theme, and action only what God is highlighting for us. This requires wisdom, but the bottom line is, the purpose of the encounter is to grow us, not weigh us down.

Tuck Your Cloak into Your Belt

Stewarding our encounters and all the ways the King's prophetic voice speaks to us, begins with tucking our cloak into our belt, which brings increase and acceleration to what God is releasing to you.

> *Then the Lord gave special strength to Elijah. He tucked his cloak into his belt and ran ahead of Ahab's chariot all the way to the entrance of Jezreel* (1 Kings 18:46 NLT).

I keep hearing this phrase over and over lately, "Tuck your cloak into your belt." It's a prophetic "now word" for the season, but it's also truth that applies to hearing and stewarding the King's prophetic voice in all the ways He speaks to us. Taking hold of this truth will help you apply God's prophetic voice in your life.

Let me explain.

Recently, I woke up from a dream saying out loud, "Tuck your cloak into your belt." I didn't hear a 3-point message on what that meant. I just heard a phrase, which I knew came straight from the Bible, in First Kings 18.

The first step to stewarding God's prophetic voice is *research*. So I reread First Kings 18, taking particular notice of verse 46 where it says, *"He tucked his cloak into his belt"* and then using credible sources, I researched what that phrase meant in biblical times.

To give you the context, the prophet Elijah just had a show-down of power intercession and raw courage to stand in the face of intimidation. The false prophets were just killed off and God gave His people an invitation to be fully surrendered to Him. Then Elijah decreed an end to the drought and prayed until he saw the beginnings of change. He encouraged himself by listening to what God was saying, not focusing on the circumstances. He heard *"the sound of heavy rain"* long before he saw the small cloud on the horizon (1 Kings 18:41 NIV). There's so much in that right there!

After Elijah sees the breakthrough of the small cloud, the Bible says that the power of God came upon him, and Elijah famously ran faster than a chariot to his destination, Jezreel, which was about 20 miles away! Acceleration came upon him.

This is about to come on the body of Christ in this season in unprecedented ways.

Before Elijah took off running and supernatural acceleration came upon him, he tucked his actual cloak into his belt. Because of the clothing of the day, before men could run they had to pull up their long cloak out of the way and tuck it into their belts.

A cloak, or mantle as some translations say, also represents anointing. In short, it represented the call over Elijah's life and the anointing he was graced with. His destiny and call in God is a simple way to put it.

In Scripture the belt often represents "the truth." Ephesians 6:14 (NIV) says, *"Stand firm then, with the belt of truth buckled around your waist…"* and is listed as part of the full armor of God (Ephesians 6:10-17). The Bible is our foundation of truth, and the truth of God is our guardrail in life.

Stewarding Is Refining and Recalibrating

Elijah's act of tucking his anointing into truth was a practical act allowing him to run fast, and it also spoke of a spiritual truth that tidying up our ministry and lives is necessary before acceleration comes. Prophetically speaking, to tuck our cloak into our belt symbolizes tidying up any aspect of our lives that will make us trip when the season heats up and things happen faster.

The wisdom we can take from this is that heavy rain is upon us, and acceleration is coming. It's a recalibration and refining season. It's time to get healed up and strengthened. It's a time to recalibrate, refine our focus, and reset our heart on the things that matter most so as to be ready for what is coming. There is a window right now to upgrade the practical and the spiritual foundations, so that processes are simplified and ready for the coming increase.

It means doing the work now to sort out the behind-the-scenes aspects in our ministries, families, and personal walk with the Lord, and breaking free from endless procrastination. If we are not focused on the right things now, when acceleration hits we will run fast in the wrong direction. Or if we have not fortified practical systems, healed broken places, and streamlined our lives to divine purpose, we will trip as we try and keep up with all God is pouring out.

Tucking your cloak into your belt is practical stewardship, which includes the following:

- Re-ignite your relationship with God and put actions and healthy habits in place that build strength of connection to God.

- Rearrange your life and commitments to make time for God.

- Repent of hidden sin and get healed. Ask for help to do that if needed. Remember, there's no shame in getting help to be set free.

- Clean your filters. Let go of past hurt, offenses, disappointments, and unforgiveness. This stuff weighs you down and will affect your future destination if not dealt with. We benefit from a "clean heart."

- Slay the giant of procrastination and finally do what God is speaking to you about. Do the hard things you've been putting off.

- Refine your focus. First, focus on Him, then refine your focus for this season to prioritize what God is speaking about.

- Recalibrate your purpose and guard your time so you can prioritize what matters more in the season. Say no to others, so you can say yes to Him.

- Readjust your use of time. Stop wasting time on what doesn't matter moving forward. It's not that some things aren't good, it's just that they aren't helpful for where you are heading.

- Plan for harvest and "heavy rain." Turn faith expectations into plans.

- Get oil. Build and fortify your faith now. You will need the oil to keep your lamp burning. Your relationship with Jesus must be prioritized. Implement personal prayer and word upgrades.

- Obey quickly. Take Mary's advice, the mother of Jesus, who said, *"Do whatever He tells you"* (John 2:5 NIV). We're approaching days when the consequences of hearing and doing will be magnified.

- Take advantage of the open doors God provides as pathways for provision and promise. Once you know it's a "God door," be bold.

- Prepare for the faith expectations God is stirring. Turn faith expectations into plans and practical processes, and plan for the harvest God is speaking to you about.

My encouragement to you is to take the time to evaluate what tucking your cloak into your belt looks like for you. Just like Elijah ran faster than the most advanced vehicle of his day, you will outrun the best the world has to offer and rapidly establish new breakthrough.

This process of stewarding what God is saying to you through His prophetic voice gives you tools to practically steward the mystical. This will transform your life and call.

Practical Stewarding of God's Prophetic Symbolism

Moving forward in stewarding God's prophetic voice in your life, there are foundational truths that bring increase. When you have an encounter or God speaks to you in a creative way, the following are two keys to stewarding the prophetic voice of God in your midst: research and awareness.

1. Research.

When you have an encounter, seek further understanding from God. Research the focus of the encounter. Ask what the picture or symbol means. Lean in and look for details in the vision or dream and ask the Holy Spirit if there is anything else He wants to show you. Sometimes we can miss additional insight by simply not leaning in for more at the time of the encounter.

When it comes to prophetic symbolism, the practical process of researching the symbols God uses or is highlighting will give you personal insight. As you research facts about the symbol, God will often highlight prophetic understanding.

For instance, a few years ago God kept highlighting flamingos to me. I saw them everywhere in the natural for a season, and I had dreams and visions of them chasing me down! At first I had no idea what God was saying—all I knew was that God was bringing them to my attention to say something.

As I researched facts about flamingos, God gave me profound prophetic insight. This became a word for me about revival fire and mentoring women. All from seeing flamingoes! Your research of prophetic symbolism is stewardship of God's prophetic voice.

2. Turn aside and take notice of God's supernatural revelation.

Moses and the burning bush encounter gives us much insight into how to steward a supernatural encounter by turning toward God and making space for Him, as recorded in Exodus 3. We can over-spiritualize stories from the Bible sometimes and miss the "realness" of what actually happened.

For context, Moses was just doing his job, tending his father-in-law's sheep. He had a job in the family business, which no doubt wasn't his passion as it was certainly not how he grew up, but it paid the bills and kept food on the table. The Scriptures tell us that he was in the wilderness, which probably summed up Moses' life quite succinctly at this point in time. He was being faithful where he was, but clearly wasn't in the sweet spot of all he was called to do and be.

STEWARDING TRANSITION LOOKS LIKE FAITHFULNESS UNTIL GOD SPEAKS THE NEXT THING.

I can only imagine the thoughts, prayer times, and questions that plagued Moses' heart as he spent day after day alone in the open spaces. Remember, he was a pioneer, leader, political activist, religious disrupter, friend of God, prayer warrior, nation reformer, apostle, prophet, and eventual deliverer of millions. The stirrings of destiny would no doubt be compelling him to seek God and also question his current situation.

Like so many of us, Moses was in the classic transition season. Moses wasn't where he had been, but not yet where he was called to be. He was faithful in the transition, and productive with what he knew until God interrupted and got his attention through unusual manifestations (see Exodus 3).

The supernatural activates destiny and its value should never be diminished. Your encounters can change your life! The King's prophetic voice is not an add-on, it's a catalyst of transformation. Supernatural manifestations and encounters, when sourced from God, can activate your destiny, just as the burning bush encounter activated Moses' destiny! The encounter itself will often impart anointing for what God is calling you to.

Supernatural encounters can change nations when stewarded properly. Encounters can be very significant! More than a million people were delivered from captivity and tyranny because one man paid attention to an angel in an unusual burning fire on a walk at work!

How did Moses respond to the King's prophetic voice? Well, certainly, stopping and turning aside to see the fire of God was key. The burning bush was not Moses' everyday, normal way of encountering God and could not be ignored. Ignoring the burning bush would have meant missing what the very voice of God had to say to a nation!

God's prophetic voice may appear in strange ways—and we must not minimize the importance of honoring and turning aside when God chooses to speak to us in encounters. His voice might appear strange, but it is not insignificant. This is stewardship of the King's prophetic voice.

I wonder how often we have missed significant revelation because we minimized, or didn't turn aside, when God spoke to us in a way we weren't used to hearing Him speak.

To be clear, yes this does require discernment and maturity, but if you are serving the Lord, you can trust Him to lead you into wisdom. Sadly, too often people have more faith in the ability of the devil to deceive them than in God's power to speak and confirm His word to them.

Let your heart rest in this truth:

> *Let me ask you this: Do you know of any father who would give his son a snake on a plate when he asked for a serving of fish? Of course not! Do you know of any father who would give his daughter a spider when she had asked for an egg? Of course not! If imperfect parents know how to lovingly take care of their children and give them what they need, how much more will the perfect heavenly Father give the Holy Spirit's*

fullness when his children ask him (Luke 11:11-13 TPT).

You can trust God to give you good things when you are seeking Him. We have a perfect heavenly Father who desires to give us the Holy Spirit's fullness. If you are asking God for more, and seeking God for understanding of spiritual things, you can trust Him to grow you and show you His ways.

Discerning Is Stewardship

Discernment is not grown by studying the devil and his ways. Discernment is grown by studying God, His Word, and His ways. How is that accomplished? Immerse yourself in God, the Bible, healthy spiritual community, and actively build your relationship with Him. This is how you grow in maturity and discernment.

John 10:27 (NKJV) says, *"My sheep hear My voice, and I know them, and they follow Me."* God's children hear from God and recognize His voice. God is saying, if you are Mine, you will hear and recognize My voice, and it will cause you to follow Me. God has great plans for you, friend. And He's very good at communicating them to you. Make room to search out and steward what He shows you, as this brings the increase.

Our "Burning Bush Encounter"

I would be amiss to not mention the "burning bush encounter" in our lives and how God used an angel to launch our ministry, Pour It Out Ministries.

As briefly mentioned in Chapter 3, my husband and I were awakened in the middle of the night by a 10-foot angel on the end of our bed. This encounter completely changed our lives and marked us with healthy fear of the Lord (you can read about this more fully in my book, *The King's Decree*). From this encounter, we sought the Lord for understanding, leaning in and stewarding His voice. God spoke and gave us a mandate from Zechariah 4 to *"pour out the oil"* of His presence and power in the nations, which led to the birthing of Pour It Out Ministries.

My point is simple: an "unusual" supernatural encounter completely changed our lives and called us into a mandate for revival and souls. We could have said, "Wow, God, that was a cool encounter" and left it at that, and it would have been wonderful. But in seeking God and stewarding the encounter, our new season of ministry was birthed.

I continue to receive revelation from Zechariah 4 that has led to thousands of salvations and healings. It was more than an angelic visitation—it was a burning bush that released a call from the Lord. Stewardship of the encounter was key.

Stewarding the King's prophetic voice can, and will, change your life. It's meant to!

Practical Keys to Steward Your Encounter Summary

1. Turn aside and take notice when something is clearly not usual, normal, or is supernatural. Don't miss the burning bush moment.
2. Take time to research any deeper meaning and prophetic symbolism.

3. Tuck your cloak into your belt and apply the message to your life in practical ways.

4. Don't rush the process. Allow the Holy Spirit time to unfold what He's revealing.

5. Sometimes the most obvious meaning is what God is saying. Don't overcomplicate it.

6. If after all this you don't know the purpose, interpretation, or meaning of an encounter, keep a note of it and shelve it for another time. You may find years later God will shine light on something from another season, so don't get stuck or overwhelmed in the process of working it out. You can trust the Holy Spirit to lead you into progressive revelation.

7. Make preparations for the faith expectations God has given you. This stewards His voice.

Mentoring Moment with the King

- How has the King's prophetic voice impacted your ministry call and life?

- What progressive revelation are you still receiving from past times God has spoken to you?

- Is there some research you need to do to understand your encounters more?

- What does turning aside look like for you in this season?

- Describe in practical ways what "tuck your cloak into your belt" means in this season to you.

■ Taking note of the main themes God is talking to you about, what are your faith expectations for this season?

■ What preparations can you put in place to be ready for the faith expectations God has given you? Are there practical ways you can better steward God's prophetic voice?

Activation Prayer

King Jesus, I desire to steward the burning bush encounters, and tuck my cloak into my belt. I ask for discernment upgrades to see and know You in the common and the uncommon. Help me reorder my life to the heartbeat of all You are saying, and recalibrate my prophetic "knower" to lean in when You're in my midst. Saturate my heart with the atmosphere of Heaven, and infuse me with contagious fire. Amen.

8

WHERE'S THAT IN THE BIBLE?

THIS CHAPTER FOCUSES ON THE UNUSUAL, CREATIVE, AND supernatural ways God spoke during Bible times. When referring to hearing God's prophetic voice or unusual supernatural encounters, people often ask, "Where's that in the Bible?" It's a great question, and easily answered in a general way. The simple answer being, from cover to cover in the Bible God uses His supernatural ways and prophetic voice to reach His people with His messages and display His glory.

Sometimes it's not curiosity that sparks this question, but rather a predisposed acceptance that God would not do something *that* supernatural in our world today. Or while some acknowledge God spoke through prophetic symbolism in Bible days, they *forget* He is the same God today and discard similar accounts of God's prophetic voice now. I've often found God's supernatural voice and ways to be outside my comfort zone at times, sometimes "messy" by human standards, and certainly deliberately faith-stretching.

A Dream Brought Her to Church

In our Pour It Out Ministry School, over the years we have taught many on the prophetic and hearing God. We've journeyed with some people who had been clairvoyants in the past, and had since encountered God, received Jesus as Lord, been delivered and now were on a new journey to hear the voice of God through clean filters. We've had to train these people how *not* to hear from a dark source, and how to recognize God's voice instead. As you can imagine, this was messy at times. For everyone's benefit, this process involved establishing clean filters and pure pathways, which included healing, deliverance, repentance, training, and protocol. All that took time. But during this beautiful journey, one thing was constant—God found a way to talk to each precious person, even in their darkest moments and most deceived seasons. Jesus' love can and will chase down anyone with a seeking heart for Him.

One woman who had been a clairvoyant ended up in church after having a very vivid dream God gave her. In the dream, she saw the church building and name, and the door of the church. As she walked through the door, she saw my husband who gave her a hug. This dream so deeply impacted her that she googled the name she saw, Pour It Out Ministries, and discovered we were meeting in her city. She had a lot going on and was fearful of attending because the enemy tried to convince her that was a bad idea.

However, the dream wouldn't leave her alone. She was having health issues, and so she courageously came to the building she had seen in her dream. She told us that when she arrived, everything in her was telling her to run the other way, and the only thing that caused her to walk through the door was that it looked just like in her dream.

As she entered, she saw the man she had seen in her dream, Ben, my husband and senior leader. She walked straight up to him, just as in her dream, and Ben embraced her in a hug and welcomed her, just as it had happened in her dream. She said there was a war inside her, but that hug felt like home. Ben sat near her as she worshipped and joined in that day, assuring her she was welcome and God loved her.

At the end of the service, I will never forget what unfolded. This woman came forward for prayer, gave her life to Jesus, was delivered, received prayer for healing, and turned into a blubbering mess as we prayed for her to be filled with the Holy Spirit. It wasn't a quiet prayer time. It wasn't a comfortable prayer time. But it was a powerful prayer time. I'll never forget the joy on her face after giving her life to Jesus when she kept crying and saying, "He's real, He's real, He's really real!" I'll also never forget how God broke into this clairvoyant's life with a dream and sent her to church. God's prophetic voice is so very creative and loving!

Golden Oil

One time a hurting guy came to church because of an unusual supernatural experience. He was riding in a public bus and looking out the window. As the bus passed by our church, he saw golden oil dripping down from the roof all over the building. He didn't know what he was seeing or what the building was, or if anyone else saw the dripping golden oil. Astounded, he later asked a friend, who just happened to attend our church, about the building and was told it was a church. Interestingly, golden oil is spoken of in Zechariah 4, the oil of His presence that keeps the lamp stand (church) burning, which is the mandate over Pour It Out Ministries—to pour out the oil of His presence and power in the nations! God is cool. This man courageously showed up at church that next weekend—to the building where he saw the golden oil dripping down from the roof. Praise God. He found freedom that day and gave his heart to Jesus. All this from a supernatural vision of golden oil. God is out of the box! The King's prophetic voice is not boring or dull. God is chasing hard after hearts with His love, even in ways that look unusual or different from how some think God "should" speak and act.

Poured Out the Wine

Another time, a woman heard God's still small voice very clearly one day. God said to her, "Pour it out." She had been an avid wine collector and had recently received an order. She thought God was asking her to pour out the wine; so amazingly, she went outside and poured out the not-cheap wine on the ground. As she told us, she still had a holy frustration about what God was saying to her, even after she "poured it out." So she researched on the Internet to gain further insight and discovered Pour It Out ministries met not too far from where she lived. She attended a service, found like-spirited people, and eventually joined our ministry school. Later, she had a profound encounter lying on the floor with "the real Jesus" during the Pineapple Revival that transformed her relationship with God. Her life was forever changed by the King's prophetic voice speaking to her in an unusual way.

So Where Is That in the Bible?

Imagine if one of those precious people were asked, "Well, where's that in the Bible? I don't see golden oil dripping down buildings anywhere, or clairvoyants dreaming of buildings, or people having dreams and hearing words like "pour it out," and then pouring out bottles of wine in the Bible.

All three stories are about real people who found God in real but unusual ways, but you'd be hard-pressed to find their exact stories in the Bible.

What you will find in the Bible though are stories of Jesus turning water to wine, expensive perfume poured out on Jesus' feet, visions of golden oil pouring down two gold pipes (Zechariah 4:12), and people who were led to safe places in dreams like Joseph, Jesus' father. You will find prophetic words that led people to specific places like the "Potter's house" to hear a word from the Lord (Jeremiah 18:1-2). Those with eyes to see and ears to hear will see the handiwork of God through the pages of the Bible, urging us to believe.

The King's prophetic voice is woven through the entire Bible urging us, compelling us, to see Him as He is. A loving Father who speaks in supernatural, miraculous, powerful ways to a world He loves.

Jesus Did More Than Is Recorded in the Bible

And there are also many other things that Jesus did, which if they were written one by one, I suppose that even the world itself could not contain the books that would be written. Amen (John 21:25 NKJV).

The Passion Translation says, *"Jesus did countless things that I [John] haven't included here."* John, His disciple and best friend, is saying he saw so much more than he's written about. No doubt these "many other things" includes countless miraculous healings, resurrections, supernatural encounters of every kind, and people finding faith in Jesus, the Son of God, in unusual ways.

This verse, among other things, tells us that if you are looking specifically for every exact miracle and encounter to be found in the Bible, you won't find it. What you *will* find, though, is the God of "all things are possible"! The point is, Jesus did many more miracles than is written down in the Bible, and the Bible was never intended to limit our faith to what has already been done, but rather, catapult our faith to believe for what we haven't seen yet.

Fruit Doesn't Always Grow Overnight

So, it begs the question, how do you discern if something is from God that you haven't experienced before or is not specifically mentioned in the Bible? You need to look for fruit. What is the fruit of how God is speaking? Keep in mind, fruit doesn't grow overnight, and sometimes you need to allow time for fruit to grow.

Good questions to ask to discern if the experience is from God:

- Is this pointing to Jesus?
- Is God using this?
- Is there observable fruit? What is the fruit?
- Do I sense God speaking through this?

- Do I recognize God's voice in this?
- Is God's presence on this and does it resonate with my spirit?

THE BIBLE IS FULL OF UNUSUAL, SUPERNATURAL STORIES

I encourage you to look up and read the following unusual and strange supernatural stories, as recorded in the Bible (as you read take note of how "supernatural" the Bible is):

- Genesis 5:19-24. Enoch, a godly man suddenly disappears from the earth. He is translated by God to be with Him without dying.
- Exodus 4:6-7. Moses' hand suddenly becomes infected with leprosy, then suddenly is restored to normal again after putting his hand back inside his cloak.
- Exodus 7:10-12. Moses' brother's staff suddenly turns into a snake and swallows up all the staffs of the Egyptian sorcerers. The Bible records, *"Aaron's staff swallowed up their staffs"* (NIV), meaning a stick ate other sticks!
- Exodus 7:19-24. Egypt's entire national water supply system—streams, canals, ponds, and reservoirs—is turned from water into blood at Moses' command.
- Exodus 13:21-22. A pillar of cloud, a literal cloud, led the Israelites in a desert by the day,

and a pillar of fire led them at night. The cloud and the fire were their GPS.

- Exodus 14:21-29. The Red Sea separates creating a pathway for an entire nation to escape certain death and migrate to a new land. More than one million people walked through a sea on dry ground, and then the sea closed again and swallowed the soldiers pursuing them. Imagine that!

- Exodus 16:14-15. Manna, supernatural food, appeared every morning to feed over a million people. The manna sustained an entire nation. This supernatural food rotted every day, to prevent hoarding; except before Sabbath when it would last for two days allowing for rest and worship of God. Quail also supernaturally appeared to feed the people at night. This means food just appeared for a nation!

- Exodus 19:16-18. A very loud supernatural trumpet blast was heard, and the mountain trembled violently at the same time. All the people saw supernatural fire and smoke.

- Numbers 17:8. Aaron's staff, basically a stick, suddenly grows buds and blossoms.

- Numbers 20:7-11. Moses strikes a rock with his staff and water flows out from a rock, enough for a whole nation and their livestock to drink.

- Numbers 21:6-9. The sick are healed while looking at a brass snake on a pole. Wow, that is definitely supernaturally unusual.

- Joshua 6. Instructions are given to a nation to silently march around an enemy city for six days, and on the seventh day, march around it seven times, and then shout. As the nation shouted, the walls of the city of Jericho fell to the ground. Marching and shouting were the weapons of God's choice.

- Joshua 10:12-14. The sun and moon literally stood still in the sky to allow for longer daylight for a battle where God secured a greater victory for His people.

- Judges 7:13-25. God helps Gideon win a battle even though he is impossibly outnumbered. God gave a dream to the enemy army that put fear in the enemy's hearts.

- 1 Samuel 3:2-10. The audible voice of God speaks to a young boy three times and calls him into full-time ministry. God's audible voice changed this young man's life forever.

- 1 Kings 17:2-6. Elijah, a man of God, is fed by ravens. Yes, birds bring him food.

- 1 Kings 18:41-46. As acceleration comes on Elijah he runs faster than the fastest vehicle of the day. This is like a person prophesying then running faster than a sports car on a freeway.

- 1 Kings 19:5-8. Elijah is fearing for his life and an angel provides supernatural food which sustains him for 40 days and nights. I'd like that one to happen to me!

- 2 Kings 2:11. Elijah is taken into Heaven in a whirlwind when a chariot and horses ablaze with fire suddenly appears. People there saw it happen!

- 2 Kings 4:1-7. A multiplication miracle happens when a widow's oil supply is supernaturally refilled. That's like your wallet being replenished with cash or business supplies supernaturally replenished as they are given away.

- 2 Kings 4:32-37. A resurrection miracle brought a dead son back to life, as Elisha lay on top of the dead body.

- 2 Kings 6:16-17. A whole company of people who served Elisha had an open-eye vision of being surrounded by horses and chariots of fire. God opened their eyes to see the angelic army of the Lord surrounded them. That's a miracle I wish we could all see today.

- 2 Kings 13:20-21. After falling in a ditch on top of Elisha's dead bones, a man came back to life. Elisha's bones carried resurrection power even after he died. Can we believe to carry resurrection power while we're alive?

- 2 Kings 20:9-11. Time literally goes backward. Yes, that's wild—one for sci-fi fans!

- Daniel 2:26-45. Daniel supernaturally knows what a king's dream is and then interprets it. He tells him what God is saying.

- Daniel 3:14-30. Three young people are bound and thrown into a fiery furnace as punishment for not worshipping a government leader. They are supernaturally protected in the fire when a "fourth man," the son of God, appears. They don't even smell of smoke. What a miracle!

- Daniel 5:5. A hand supernaturally appears at a royal function and writes a message on the wall that everyone can see.

- Luke 1:11-25. An angel appears to Zechariah while on duty in the temple as a priest. When he doesn't believe what the angel tells him, he is suddenly unable to speak.

- Matthew 4:11. Angels are sent to minister to Jesus and feed Him after 40 days and 40 nights of fasting. Did you grasp that? Angels feed Jesus. Days are coming when this miracle is one to lean into for yourself.

- John 2:1-11. Jesus turns water into wine. Jesus transformed one substance into another substance.

- Luke 4:28-30. Jesus supernaturally escapes from an angry mob who wants to hurt Him. That's one way to escape persecution.

- Matthew 8:23-26. Jesus speaks to a raging storm and the weather immediately changes. Many have prayed and seen storms dissipate and tornadoes shift course. These miracles should stir our faith for creation miracles.

- Luke 9:10-17. A multiplication miracle was witnessed when 5,000-plus people are fed from just two loaves and five fish.

- John 6:19. Jesus walked on the water.

- Matthew 17:24-27. Money appears in the mouth of a fish to pay a tax. Everybody likes that one! But imagine your mortgage money appearing in a bird's beak in your backyard!

- John 11:43-44. Lazarus had been dead four days but is raised to life by Jesus. This literally is one of my favorite supernatural miracles!

- Luke 22:50-51. A man's ear is cut off with a sword; when Jesus places it on the man's head, it's restored instantly. A medical miracle!

- Matthew 27:51-53. Jesus' crucifixion caused an earthquake; dead people were raised to life and came out of the tombs and walked around Jerusalem where many people saw them alive. Resurrection power is powerful!

- John 20:1-9 and all the Gospels. The resurrection of Jesus back from the dead. All the gospels cover this miracle. Jesus conquers death. Our

King Jesus has conquered the grave and consequently His voice speaks forth life.

- Acts 5:18-20. An angel releases the apostles from prison after being locked up for preaching the gospel.

- Acts 8:39-40. Philip is translated—supernaturally taken from one place to another—to tell a man from another nation about Jesus. That's one way to preach the gospel in shut-down nations and locked borders!

- Acts 9:3-7. Jesus Himself appears to Saul in a vision, a light from heaven flashed, and it changes everything! Saul stops persecuting believers and actually goes into ministry serving Jesus. That's a great one to pray over people, especially ungodly leaders. Dreams and visions that turn their lives around.

- Acts 19:11-12. The Bible says God worked unusual miracles through Paul. Ever wonder about praying over objects and then sending them to the sick? At the Pineapple Revival, people brought pineapples that we prayed over and they took them back to their church as an act of faith. Where's that in the Bible? Right there in Acts 19!

- 2 Corinthians 12:1-6. Paul has a vision of Heaven that deeply affects him. He is *caught up to paradise and heard inexpressible things* (NIV).

This is one for those who have heavenly encounters and visions.

- ▪ Revelation 4:1-11. John, Jesus' best friend, has a vision of the future days to come.

I could go on listing supernatural encounters recorded in the Bible, as this is far from an exhaustive list of manifestations and prophetic occurrences of the King's prophetic voice, but it reveals an excellent overview of just how wild, unusual, and profoundly "out there" some of the ways God communicated were, and are.

DISCERNING THE KING'S PROPHETIC VOICE MUST BE BIBLICAL—AND BIBLICAL MEANS SUPERNATURAL!

Many of us have a personal *grid*, or a biblical normal, by which we evaluate encounters and supernatural signs. Often it's based on our experiences or lack of experiences. Sometimes it is based on what we think the Bible says, without realizing just how full of wildly supernatural encounters the Bible actually is. Biblical indeed means supernatural.

Of course, the Bible is full of everyday people who encountered God in somewhat "normal" ways too, and we are encouraged to keep the main message. However, the more common, normal, everyday interactions with God does not invalidate the sometimes less common, or more unusual, supernatural interactions with God.

By the way, we have noticed that unchurched people expect a God who is supernatural and speaks in out-of-the-box ways. They're expecting that God has supernatural solutions! Of course, "weird" doesn't automatically mean God is the source of an encounter—discernment is needed. On the other hand, "weird" can mean it is God! So what are the perimeters? Use your discernment as the Holy Spirit gives peace, or if you have a lack of peace—and be connected to the body of Christ as *"by their fruits you will know them"* (read Matthew 7:15-20 NKJV).

AND SO, "WHERE'S THAT IN THE BIBLE?"

The King's prophetic voice never violates the Bible, it is established that His prophetic voice is biblically sound and is supernatural! If by asking, "Where's that found in the Bible?" we mean where in the Bible does it record stories that are wildly supernatural, radically unusual, and stretch our faith for what is possible—the answer is, from cover to cover in the Bible!

The real question is, has the God of the Bible, who speaks through His prophetic voice today, stretched our faith to believe for more?

Mentoring Moment with the King

- Which Bible stories inspire you and stretch your faith to see similar things?
- Write one specific supernatural breakthrough you are believing for in this season, and turn it into a prayer.
- Has reading these biblical accounts of God speaking and moving stretched and stirred you? How is God making you hungry for more than you've yet experienced?

■ How will these Scriptures affect your prayer life and faith expectations?

Activation Prayer

Lord, grow me, stretch me, mold me, convict me, stir me, revive me, and use me! The call on my life requires faith for what I haven't seen yet. I ask for miracles, signs, and wonders in my life as I share the Good News with people, as recorded in the Bible. Fill me with excitement and expectation of good as You speak to me and move in my life and circumstances. Give me contagious joy as I encounter You, and believe You for more than I've yet experienced. Amen.

9

HOW THE PROPHETIC VOICE OF GOD LOOKS AND SOUNDS

M ANY HAVE EXPERIENCED GOD SPEAKING IN WHAT WE describe as an unusual, prophetic, or supernatural way. Remember, though, all the ways God speaks is supernatural, as He is supernatural. But some ways are more common and more understood by the greater body of Christ.

The following is a broad overview of ways God's prophetic voice can interact with us. Use this list to process through different ways God has spoken to you, or as a guide to how the King's prophetic voice can speak to others.

How God Speaks Guide

As you read through this guide, take time to ask yourself, *Have I heard God speak to me through any of these ways? What are the most common ways God speaks to me? Are there ways God speaks to me from this list that I find easier to process and interpret than others? How has God used these in my life to grow and lead me?*

Under each example of how God speaks, note what this looks like in your life and where God is stretching you the most.

1. Written Word of God: the Bible, the logos word of God in written form.

2. A rhema word through the Bible: When God highlights His written logos word to you and it comes alive and leaps off the page; this is now a rhema, spoken "utterance" word to you from the Bible. It's God's Word, but He spoke it to you personally in a moment.

3. Audible voice of God: hearing His voice speak clearly outside of you through your physical ears. You could also hear music, sounds, instruments, and creative sounds like unlocking or fire crackling, angels singing etc., with your natural ears.

4. Inner audible voice of God: this can sound like hearing a clear voice from inside you with clarity and ease, and it seems to interrupt your thoughts. It can be soft or loud.

5. Inner witness: A knowing, sensing, or resonating in your spirit about something. Sensing the Holy Spirit breathe on something, confirming yes or no, or urging you forward in a particular direction or decision.

6. Still small voice: A knowing, revelation, or inspired thought, concept, or idea that is highlighted to you, or a sudden God-thought that

drops in your heart and resonates. Entire thoughts or ideas can "drop" in a sudden knowing.

7. Dreams: Can be faint or strong and clear like watching a movie scene. Some dreams are quickly forgotten if not immediately recalled on waking, and others can be replayed in your mind's eye like remembering a movie.

8. Visions: There are several different ways God can speak to you through visions. Some examples:

    ▪ Open-eyed vision. You're awake, and see a vision appear in front of you clearly—as real as you are seeing something with your natural eyes.

    ▪ A vision while awake but seeing something in your spirit (or could be described as in your mind's eye). This could be very clear, or faint and sometimes needs pressing into for greater clarity with the Lord.

    ▪ Flash vision. A sudden vision that is only seen for a split second, but could either be just a picture, or an entire scene in a moment. This could be seen on your inside or outside.

    ▪ Trance. Like an open-eyed vision except rather than seeing something in front of you, you are taken into the vision scene, as if you are somewhere else. You are experiencing it like you are actually there.

- Impressions in your spirit that you see, and may be accompanied by an immediate knowing, sensing, or feeling something.

9. Hearing sounds that are natural or supernatural, but they were supernatural in origin. For instance, angels worshipping, drums, thunder, laughing, bells, doors opening, chains breaking, or hearing lines from well-known songs. You could hear instruments, creative noises, or repetitive sounds like fire alarms, marching of an army, or wind blowing through the trees.

10. Prophetic symbolism: God highlighting something in the natural such as an everyday object, picture, or symbol that speaks to you prophetically. God uses this object in a symbolic way to bring a deeper message. For example, a cactus blooming, a lion roaring, pineapples, church bells ringing, keys, flamingoes fishing, a specific vehicle, a house renovation, or an elephant stomping.

It could also be when God breathes on something—a moment, event, date or object—it is to draw your attention to it. It could be a piece of art, a song you hear while driving, a movie that suddenly feels prophetic, an object you see that captures your attention, a work situation

God draws your attention to, walking past a map, words of a friend or sermon that resonate, a rainbow, a social media post or news story that leaps out at you, a phrase on a billboard, a number sequence such as 1111 or 911, numbers or letters on a license plate that God highlights, or a road sign, etc. In all these examples, you sense God speaking to you from something natural that suddenly grips you.

Repetitive symbolic highlighting: Much like all these examples but you are seeing the same thing over and over. You begin to be aware that God is using repetition to speak to you. This can include words, signs, animals, numbers, or times. For instance, repeatedly seeing turtles, hearing someone's name come up constantly in conversation, a particular color you keep noticing, the same number sequence such as 2222 or 333, suddenly waking up at the same time night after night for a season, a word or name is consistently highlighted to you, or for a season it seems every restaurant seats you at the same table number, or you're given the same hotel room number, suddenly being upgraded consistently, or noticing as you are brought water when out eating the glasses keep overflowing or spilling. In all these examples, the repetition draws your attention and highlights a deeper meaning.

11. Signs and wonders: Supernatural manifestations or unusual occurrences that intercept the earthly realm with the glory realm. For example, the physical manifestation of things like oil, honey, rain falling, fire appearing, feathers, gold teeth appearing in people's mouths, diamonds or gold dust, a glory cloud, or bright lights that flash in the room like lightning. These are just a few of many, many different ways God might manifest signs and wonders.

12. Angelic visitations and encounters. This can be either via an actual visitation of an angel, or can also happen in a dream or vision. Again this can be in dreams, visions, an impression, or a knowing with eyes open or closed.

13. Highlighting past memories or encounters with God: God uses our memories, bringing to your attention a memory of a past time God spoke, or reminding you of something in the past that speaks prophetically to a current situation.

14. Fragrances and supernatural smells: Fragrances that supernaturally appear and have a prophetic meaning or are associated with angelic or supernatural activity. Using a fragrance to release a prophetic word such a frankincense or smoke from a fire. For example, supernaturally smelling the crispness of air after the rain, or smelling honey, roses, or fresh bread baking.

15. Nature and creation: God using natural surroundings or creation to highlight or speak a prophetic message to you. Natural phenomena such as winds, forest fires, the expanse of an oak tree's branches, the birth of twins, or a rainbow after a storm could all be used to convey prophetic revelation. For example, God highlighting the depth or time of an earthquake, a strong wind blowing inside a building or suddenly whipping through a region, rainbows appearing in unusual places such as indoors or inside cars, or God speaking through a double rainbow. God can speak through bees swarming, a ladybug, a bird's song, a praying mantis that seems to usher in a call to pray, a king (exceptionally high) tide, the name of a storm, or a waterfall or a particularly glorious sunrise. An animal could be used to do something that seems unusual and draws your attention, such as a fox that keeps appearing at your back door, butterflies that suddenly appear for a season, or doves that suddenly keep flying into your home.

16. Everyday life or normal experiences and routines that become a modern prophetic parable. God uses normal life situations and circumstances, as He highlights and breathes life on these moments to use them to bring a parabolic message of a truth to us. For example,

watching your child learn to walk, focusing a camera, reading a map, or cleaning the house and the Holy Spirit highlights this and uses the process to speak a prophetic message to you.

Understanding the Ways God Most Often Speaks to You

This list is not exhaustive; rather, it is an overview of how God can speak that should prompt you to remember and take note of how God speaks to you. Take a moment and think if there are other ways He speaks to you, or what are the most common prophetic signs God is currently using to speak to you. Take note of themes and messages from the King's prophetic voice in this season. Are there examples used that prompted you to remember times when God spoke that way you had forgotten about? Write your own mental list of your favorite ways God talks to you, and past encounters that helped you grow, and brought wisdom or fresh impartation and anointing.

Get Ready for a New Wave of the Supernatural

I realize that many of the examples I've used to describe different ways God can speak are, to some, controversial or stretching. We don't serve anyone well, least of all prophetic people, by avoiding the more controversial ways God communicates for the sake of not ruffling religious feathers. We are entering days when proper is giving way to power, and increasingly we will see powerful manifestations of the miraculous that we don't have adequate words for. We haven't been this way before, which means we will see things we haven't seen before. It seems prudent then, to at the least, get used to being comfortable with being uncomfortable as God expands our expectations.

Of course, we don't need to have experienced more unusual expressions of God's voice to have relationship with Him. However, it is equally true that one person's expression of hearing God does not invalidate another's expression of hearing God, even if vastly different from themselves. The Word of God is our guide and safeguard.

A new wave of the miraculous and supernatural is upon us; it will cause the world to look in awe. God is supernatural; and if we think we've seen it all, we are in for a shock. The following quote from Ben, my husband, I think sums it up well: "If we want to do ministry strictly biblically and like Jesus, we better get ready for weird, wild, controversial, radical, and supernatural."

Mentoring Moment with the King

- What is the most common way God is speaking to you in this season, and what is His main message to you? Think about a way God has talked to you in the past that brought wisdom for a season ahead. Is God speaking to you now to prepare you for what's ahead, and how is He doing that?

- What's the most unusual or creative way God has spoken to you and what did you learn?

- How has God communicated to you that you are loved?

- What encounters bring the most joy to your heart?

- How has God been using prophetic symbolism to get your attention lately?

- Thank God for His voice in all the creative ways He has spoken to you over your life.

Activation Prayer

Thank You, God, for all the ways You talk to me. Help me to see, hear, feel, sense, know, and discern Your prophetic voice. Would You grow my capacity to hear You in the ways I'm comfortable with You speaking, and equally stretch my capacity to hear You in ways I'm not used to You speaking to me. I thank You that You are upon me to be a blessing to others, and I ask for increased boldness and wisdom to utilize Your prophetic voice as a source of blessing to those around me. Your voice is a source of blessing to me too. I'm so thankful You constantly speak to me and find creative ways to communicate your heart. Amen.

10

GOD'S SCHOOL OF THE SUPERNATURAL

ONE THING IS FOR SURE, GOD HAS NO PROBLEM SPEAKing creatively to train us in His ways. The Holy Spirit will enroll us in the School of the Supernatural, as He is committed to our growth. There will be times when you suddenly know, "Oh, this is for training! I'm in the Holy Spirit's School of the Supernatural right now." When this happens, just take the class!

> ## GOD USES THE SUPERNATURAL TO TEACH, IMPART, EQUIP, AND GROW US.

I'm going to share stories taken from my and other people's lives where God supernaturally showed up and used unusual ways to speak, teach, equip, impart, and grow. To grow in discerning the King's prophetic voice, the best teacher is the Holy Spirit. Get ready. The Holy Spirit School of the Supernatural is in session.

"Lightning" Hit Me

God used this encounter to shape me and thankfully reset me. In my early 20s, my dad encouraged me to attend a revival meeting in Sydney, Australia, featuring an internationally respected and well-known revivalist. I hadn't heard of him, though it was evident that many had when I arrived at the packed meeting. I distinctly remember the tangible thickness of the presence of God.

As I raised my hands in worship, I could actually feel a substance of something heavy and thick that I could touch and push my hands into. I'd never felt anything like it. The meeting was full of people getting saved, lots of stories of miracles, there was "an electricity" in the air, and lots and lots of laughter. The laughter seemed contagious, even raucous. I could feel God's presence, but I also had never been in a meeting anything like what I was experiencing.

As I walked out the door of the church at the end of what I now know was my first full-blown Holy Ghost revival outpouring I ever attended, I sadly, and to my shame said out loud, "That wasn't God." I decided that as this wasn't anything I had ever experienced before, and even though I had known in the moment what I was feeling and experiencing was very much God, I pronounced the whole thing as "not God."

I walked to the parking lot and slid into the back seat of my friend's car who was taking me home. Suddenly I was "hit by lightning." That's honestly the only way I can describe it. I felt like a bolt of lightning struck me and the "weight of the lightning" pushed my head down to where my feet were. I knew this was God.

I'd never felt God like this before. I was very aware in this moment that God was fierce. Not just a lamb, but also a lion. For what felt like forever, my face was literally being held down under the weight of what I would now say was the hand of God. I remember thinking in the moment, *If God doesn't let me up, I'm in trouble.* I was aware of God's power and a sudden "fear of the Lord" came upon me. I said out loud, "Alright God, that was definitely You." Immediately, the pressure lifted, and I could sit up straight. I knew God had just somehow delivered me of my own unbelieving thoughts. He had made it very clear that what I witnessed at that revival meeting may have been new to me, but it was most definitely God's power and fire that I had felt.

After sitting up, I started uncontrollably laughing. I couldn't stop! I couldn't talk. I couldn't explain to my friends what was going on or why my head had been stuck on the floor of the car. All I could do was laugh. My friend hadn't started driving yet, so I got out of the car and tried to explain to my friends what just happened.

Now not only was I laughing nonstop, I couldn't stand up straight. I was swaying and stumbling as if I was drunk. I was like all those people I had witnessed in the meeting not long ago and pronounced, "That's not God." Try as I might, I could not stop laughing and I couldn't get myself to "sober up"! I felt amazing. I felt loved. I felt on fire. I felt joy. I was overwhelmed by the presence of God like I had never been before.

I stayed "drunk in the spirit" for about three weeks. Even when I went to work at my job in the Salvation Army headquarters, I would keep breaking out in laughter. I just couldn't stop laughing. I was getting myself into pickles by answering phone calls or in meetings and people thought I was mocking them when I began laughing. I had to apologize a lot. Within a few short weeks I had resigned and packed up my life in Australia to move to New Zealand and attend Bible school at Youth With a Mission (YWAM). I *knew* I had to take the call to ministry on my life seriously. I literally got rid of my old life and bought a one-way ticket to New Zealand. There I met Ben, my husband, and we got married. My life has never been the same as God marked me with urgency to pursue Him.

But the crucial point I want to emphasize is that when I think back to that unusual encounter, I am so grateful that God stepped in, and delivered me from my unbelief. It was one big reset; I was *arrested* by the Holy Spirit. Now my husband and I are called to revival ministry. We've hosted revival, we contend for revival, and we're marked by an insatiable hunger to see nation-shaking revival that leads to billions of souls being saved and nations on fire for Jesus. The very thing I'm called to is the very thing I shamefully pronounced as "not God."

This interaction with His prophetic voice may have been out-of-the-box, and it's still wild when I think about His hand pushing my head down to the ground until I came to my senses, but I'm so thankful God stepped in and put me in the School of the Supernatural. He was teaching me, rebuking me, equipping me, and recalibrating me. Thank God He did!

When God puts you in school, it's time to learn what He wants you to know.

A Supernatural Violin Played

Years ago Ben was leading worship on his guitar, there was also a drummer, keyboard, and bass guitar in the band. The worship was amazing, but then it got even better. Suddenly I heard a violin. I opened my eyes and looked around the church building to see who was playing a violin as I knew there wasn't one in the band. I saw nobody. I figured I'd imagined it.

I closed my eyes and continued worshipping. Again I heard it loud and clear. A violin was playing in the worship. I looked around and it occurred to me that nobody else heard the violin as only I was looking around. Now I was really confused. Once again I closed my eyes and began to worship, and boom, I heard the violin again cut through and join in the worship. It was beautiful, but as I looked for where the violin was coming from, I stopped hearing it. The next time I shut my eyes to worship, something strange happened—I was hearing not just a violin, but now a woodwind instrument, other strings as well, and a full sound of glorious music worshipping along with the worship band.

This happened four times in total. Every time I heard the heavenly worship and then looked around to work out what was going on, I stopped hearing it.

DOUBT IS A DOORWAY TO UNBELIEF.

I thankfully realized God was teaching me something. God had signed me up to the School of the Supernatural, and class had already begun! After the fourth time hearing the violin, I heard the Holy Spirit speak to me, "Jodie, every time you stop listening and start doubting, doubt closes your ears and you stop hearing."

Doubt was a door to unbelief and was shutting my spiritual ears to the heavenly music. *What else was doubt preventing me from experiencing* I wondered? That was a wake-up call and a learning invitation from God. I was asking for more, and yet I realized that when more happened, I allowed doubt to steal my encounter. I doubted it was God, even though I knew in my spirit what I was hearing was heavenly and from the glory realm. Doubt unchecked is an open door to unbelief— and unbelief will not only steal your encounters with the King's prophetic voice, but stunt your faith.

This became a prayer of mine after that: "I believe, Lord, help my unbelief."

> *Jesus said to him, "If you can believe, all things are possible to him who believes." Immediately the father of the child cried out and said with tears, "Lord, I believe; help my unbelief!"* (Mark 9:23-24 NKJV)

When God puts you in school, it's because He wants to teach you something you need to know.

My TV Prophesied, "Zerubbabel!"

I shared the following story at length in my book *The King's Decree*, but to this day it's one of the more wild ways God has spoken to me and taught me truth.

Having had a long health journey of more than thirty years of intestinal disease, pressing in for keys to healing has been a common theme in my faith walk. On this occasion, I was extremely sick and the specialist told me to go to the emergency room right away, as he had grave fears for my life. Spoiler: God has brought miraculous life-saving healing to me. But on that day, I stopped and prayed before I went to the hospital, as I knew I needed God's peace and word.

Times like this show us what we really believe. I sat and prayed. The TV was on with the news in the background. I suddenly heard a static-type sound, the woman newsreader was interrupted, and I heard clearly a voice cut in and say, "ZERUBBABEL!" Then the same static sound happened again and the newsreader continued. Yes, I was shocked. But I knew right away that my TV just prophesied to me. God spoke through my TV.

I knew immediately what God was saying. Zechariah 4 is the chapter over our ministry, Pour It Out Ministries. It was a direct reference to the verse, *What are you, mighty mountain? Before Zerubbabel you will become level ground…* (Zechariah 4:7 NIV). God was provoking faith in me to use my voice, to get up off the couch and start decreeing to this supposed "mighty mountain" that it "will become level ground." The thing is, Zerubbabel was just a man, just a person, like me, like you. So God was reminding me to open my mouth and use the authority He gave me to speak to the mountains I face (see Matthew 17:20). Also, it was Zerubbabel who was given the job of rebuilding the temple! (See Zechariah 4:9 and First Corinthians 6:19-20.)

Another lesson from God! Zerubbabel's job was to rebuild the temple. If you need some rebuilding in your life, God is calling you a Zerubbabel too! Open your mouth and decree!

Command the rebuilding of God's promises into your life, family, body, and nation.

My TV spoke a word to me that day (yes it was God, but through a TV). Class that day in the School of the Supernatural gave me keys to healing, decreeing life and rebuilding. That was a good day in class! Thank God the Holy Spirit was investing in and equipping me. When the Holy Spirit puts you in school, it's to teach you something you need to know.

Supernatural Rain in Fiji

As I have ministered at times, I have seen many people feel rain who don't yet know Jesus. This happened in an outdoor market in Fiji as God led me from person to person to pray for healing, encounters, and salvation. It was amazing to see the same rain people had felt inside at church, being felt by people in the marketplace! God is moving in the marketplace, supernaturally! It certainly amazed people and made them open to prayer as they were aware something supernatural was going on.

It was a sign to me of God breaking up the fallow ground and pouring out refreshing on dry hearts in our marketplaces that were desperate for God. Many were healed and saved that day! Each person who received prayer excitedly pointed out a friend in the market who also needed prayer. Often that day I saw supernatural rain falling over someone, so I would go to them and ask if they wanted prayer. A swirl of excitement and faith broke out as miracles and salvations took place in such a fun way!

God had me in school again, teaching me to follow His lead.

Supernatural Thunder Helped a Lady Find God

In far North Queensland, a lady came to our meeting and gave her life to God after she told us that all week she had been hearing the sound of heavy rain and thunder inside her house. But it wasn't raining outside, it was sunny; and more importantly, she said she heard the sound of rain and thunder inside her house! She said at first she thought she was going crazy, but then as it happened so frequently, she felt an urgency to go to church and reconnect to God. She hadn't been in church since being a young girl, and had drifted from God. It took great courage for her to show up at church, and incredibly we were talking on First Kings 18—revival, and *"I hear the sound of heavy rain"!* Well she immediately came forward for prayer and knew God was speaking to her—and she gave her life to Jesus.

God got her attention through His prophetic voice and enrolled her in "school" that night to find Him.

God Continually Enrolls People in His School

Another lady in a small Australian town where we were ministering years ago was openly skeptical of God, of anything supernatural God did, and especially of our ministry. We know this because as we arrived at the church, she told us! Well, that same night as we preached about Jesus and revival, and told stories of miracles and healings, we included stories of people who had felt supernatural rain. We imparted faith for God of all things are possible.

I remember praying for her at the end of the meeting and having such a heart for her, as I knew she had been disappointed and hurt along the journey and was looking for God to show her more, despite being openly prickly toward us.

We heard the next day from a leader in the church saying this woman had gone home that night and felt supernatural rain in her home! It radically impacted her and did a work in her heart. She was at the hairdresser's the next day, and we were told that she couldn't stop talking about Jesus to everyone in the salon and was encouraging them to come to church with her. She had been around town telling everyone who would listen that God is alive and He does miracles today. When I saw her that night at church, I couldn't believe my eyes—she even looked different. Her eyes sparkled, and she was so happy! She brought friends too! God knows what He's doing, even if He uses unusual methods.

The Holy Spirit was showing me how He enrolls other students into the School of the Supernatural. He was also continuing to equip and stretch my heart, showing me that what I've learned was transferable and impartible to others. Faith in the Kingdom is contagious.

The school of the supernatural continues to stretch me; I'm thankful the Holy Spirit keeps enrolling us.

A Cockatoo Used by God

The following nature miracle left a lasting impact on me. I was a youth leader at the time, and a young guy who attended our weekly Bible study was wearing an openly occult symbol on his earring. I would not have brought this up, as I knew he was on a journey and already much change was going on, and my conviction was that I knew the Holy Spirit would speak to him about this. Later that night, he asked me what I thought about the earring symbol. I said I didn't like it and explained I wouldn't wear anything advertising the devil. He didn't agree with me, as he said it was just art. I didn't push him as I didn't want to argue, but made my views clear and trusted the Holy Spirit to speak. I did suggest that he pray about it and ask God what He thinks. He agreed and even prayed before he left.

I received a message the next day from him. That night when he was going to bed, he took his earring out and couldn't believe what happened next—the earring fell apart and disintegrated into small pieces in his fingers! Like dust, he said. He was amazed and said, "Well, that's my answer, God has spoken!"

But the next week he arrived with another different, openly occult symbol on his earring. I brought it up, encouraged by the last time God answered so quickly. Again he told me he didn't think there was anything wrong with it, but agreed to ask God what He thought.

Again, I received a message the next day. That night when he went home, he went outside into his backyard to say hello to their pet cockatoo, an Australian bird. As he leaned toward the bird aviary, the cockatoo stuck his head through the cage and pecked off his earring! You heard right! We didn't have any more earring conversations after that event!

That cockatoo was seriously used by God that night. None of us will ever forget God's quick and surprising answer by using a bird! I will never forget the lessons that God's School of the Supernatural has so graciously and creatively taught me over the years.

Seeing Numbers Lesson

As briefly mentioned in Chapter 6, God is getting people's attention worldwide by suddenly bringing certain numbers to their attention, or as I would say, "highlighting numbers." By this, I literally mean people are seeing the same number sequences over and over and over, to the point they *know* they are not making it up and it is not merely a coincidence.

For instance, people are waking up at the same time for nights on end, for instance 4:44 a.m. or 12:34 a.m., and then start seeing those numbers constantly in daily life. Perhaps they have made a purchase at the cafe and the total is $12.34; they top off their car's gas tank and it's $12.34. Maybe they're driving and the car license plate in front of them is 1234, then they see an address on a billboard is 1234. Or they pick up their phone and, you guessed it, it's 12:34 in the afternoon. You could probably dismiss this as coincidence, but for the next week "they" wake up again and again at exactly 12:34 a.m. By now, they realize something strange is happening. This is when many people may even start praying, "God, what the heck are You saying to me?"

I'll talk more about this, but from stories we have received, people in every nation are seeing receptive numbers, and it has become a common phenomenon. What is interesting is that God is not just speaking to believers in this way; but astoundingly, many who are not believers in Jesus yet are having the same experiences.

Some of the most common numbers people see are: 1111, 111, 2222, 911, 333, 444, 1234, 555, 316, 414, 737, 818, or 888.

You may be thinking, *Yeah, that happens to me all the time.* Or you may have thought, *That's strange,* or *That's weird, but it's not God.* But this is such a common way that God is speaking to people all across the nations right now, it is hard to ignore. Many, possibly millions are experiencing this unusual way of hearing the King's prophetic voice, so many that it's common to find people seeking God for insight.

THE SCHOOL OF THE SUPERNATURAL IS ALWAYS OPEN AND ACCEPTING STUDENTS.

To enroll in the School of the Supernatural, the only qualification you need is a teachable heart and hunger after God. Sign yourself up—apply today. Though I add, sometimes the Holy Spirit sneakily signs you up Himself and tells you later.

When God enrolls you in His school, it's to teach you something you don't already know—but you need to.

Mentoring Moment with the King

- What does the Holy Spirit School of Supernatural look like in this season for you?
- Can you identify what God is equipping and growing in you? How is He doing this?
- What lessons are you learning?
- Where have you excelled and in what areas are you still growing?

Activation Prayer

King Jesus, would You sign me up for the Holy Spirit School of Supernatural? I'm hungry, but make me more hungry, Lord. Teach me what I don't know, especially what I need to know for the season ahead. Equip me to share Your heart with others. Give me a heart for the lost and broken and those desperate for hope. And create in me a clean heart (Psalm 51:10). Expand my understanding and give me a teachable heart. Amen.

Part Two

WHAT IS GOD SAYING TO ME THROUGH PROPHETIC SYMBOLISM?

Listen and hear my voice; pay attention and hear what I say (Isaiah 28:23 NIV).

11

I SEE NUMBERS

FIRST AND FOREMOST, BEFORE WE TALK ABOUT ONE OF THE most fun and increasingly common ways the King's prophetic voice is speaking to people worldwide, it is very important for you to know that while I'm talking about hearing God speak through numbers, I do *not* endorse numerology in any form.

Numerology is *not* from God. It's vital you know that just as God speaks, so does satan and his demons—and numerology is a tool he uses to speak lies. Numerology is a form of New Age foretelling and psychic reading of your future through accessing the demonic realm. I do *not* endorse or recommend it. I strongly encourage you to stay far away from this practice. It adds only fear and confusion to your life.

This is also why I am so passionate about adding my voice to this incredible way God is speaking to people. The devil doesn't get to own numbers! God is using seeing the same number sequence repetitively to get people's attention and reach hearts of believers and unbelievers alike. We, the church, must add a godly, biblical perspective to this and help people discover Jesus, the Ultimate Communicator, who is chasing them down. To me, God speaking through bringing a number sequence to our attention is no different from any other prophetic symbolism that God may highlight and speak to you through.

What Does Seeing Numbers Mean?

So, from a Bible-based perspective, what does "seeing numbers" mean? You or a friend may have said, "I'm seeing the same number everywhere!" And wondered what on earth this could mean?

First it means that God is speaking. Numbers are just another form of God's communication, or a language if you will. The key is interpreting what God is saying through seeing repetitive number sequences such as 911, 1111, 2222, 818, 333, etc. As we talk about this, it's important to remember that numbers are just another way the King's prophetic voice is getting people's attention today. It's also a *very* common way!

My Seeing-Numbers Journey

I've been "seeing" numbers for about 15 years now. Both my husband and I had this phenomena start to happen to us at the same time. At first we thought it was just a coincidence, but as it continued to happen with ridiculous consistency and in random repetitious ways that were beyond the realms of coincidence, we started to realize that God must be talking! Even if we didn't understand what the heck He was saying, we did know that God had gotten our attention.

It started for us with seeing 1234 over and over and over. I would see this number everywhere throughout the day and night. For instance, I would consistently wake up in the night and it would be 12:34 a.m., check the time during the day and it would be 12:34 p.m., buy something random and it would cost $12:34, or see a sign or a car license plate with 1234 written on it. The numbers 1234 seemed to be chasing me down and suddenly appearing to me everywhere I looked.

Increasingly, we were both seeing 1234 highlighted every day in multiple different ways and it became a common, everyday experience. It was so common that it was getting ridiculous. We were also in a really hard season, so we were desperate to discover what this meant, and what God was saying to us.

One day as we saw "1234," through a friend we heard God say a very simple phrase that resonated deeply and brought instant peace. It was so simple, and yet so profound. We heard, "I'm lining everything up for you, as easy as ABC 1234." It almost seemed too simple, especially after many months of seeking God and the frustration of not understanding why we were seeing these numbers constantly. In the middle of all the transition and battles we were facing, I suddenly knew God was saying, through the simplicity of constantly seeing 1234, "I'm lining everything up for you, Jodie. You can trust Me." Or, in other words, alignment.

God later led me to Luke 12:34 (NKJV): *"For where your treasure is, there your heart will be also."* This spoke deeply to me that when our treasure is in God, He will be found in the midst of our search for Him. This brought great peace and confirmation. God was saying to me, "When your heart is set on seeking Me, Jodie, it is Me you will find, and I am your treasure."

Jeremiah 29:13 (NIV) says, *"You will seek me and find me when you seek me with all your heart."* I love how God wants to be found. In other words, I could trust that when I was seeking after God's heart, it is God I will find, even if His voice comes in a creative, unusual way—like seeing numbers. God was answering my heart's desire to hear from Him through four simple numbers.

SEEING A NUMBER BECAME A PROPHETIC WORD FROM GOD.

From then on, every day in that really challenging season when I would see 1234 again, it became a kiss from Heaven that immediately brought peace and reminded me that I can trust God to lead me and line everything up, even when things seemed out of control. A simple number became a prophetic word from God.

Not long after, I was in the hospital facing an extreme health battle, and at several pivotal moments I would see 1234. One night when I had been really worried and in pain, I awoke suddenly in the hospital room and checked the time—it was 12:34 a.m. I can't begin to tell you how much hope this gave me. I knew how to hear God; I had taught on hearing God's voice for many years, but in those moments when I saw 1234, it was no longer just a random coincidence or a holy frustration, it became a kiss from Heaven and a promise to hold on to.

1111 Was Chasing Me Down

Well, if I thought that was the end of that, I was wrong. I continued seeing 1234 and then all of a sudden my husband and I started seeing 1111 everywhere, I mean everywhere! It really was getting crazy, and no one we knew was having the same experience, so I was left with the same desperate prayer again, "God, what are You doing and saying?"

I'm vastly cutting this journey short, but the frustration of not knowing what God was saying caused me to constantly pray for understanding. I knew it was strange, but I also knew it was God. It seemed as if 1111 was chasing me down.

Because God had spoken so clearly about seeing 1234 and it became such a confirming word to us, and still is, I knew that seeing 1111 was also a timely word, and God would lead me.

Wake Up, Sleeping Beauty

After much prayer and seeking God about the meaning of seeing 1111 everywhere, one day I clearly heard the Holy Spirit say, "Wake up, Sleeping Beauty." I knew I was on to something, but I still didn't understand yet. I did however know that the Lord was leading me.

I read the story of Sleeping Beauty and knew God was highlighting the moment in the children's book when the prince says, "Wake up, Sleeping Beauty." From a children's story God started speaking to me about it being time to wake up. That the church, like the princess in the story, had fallen into a spiritual slumber and she needed to wake-up. I knew God was talking about His people and telling me, "It's time to wake up!"

God was talking to me about 1111 meaning it was time for the church to wake up—it's wake up hour! Over and over in my spirit every time I saw 1111, I thought, *It's time to wake up.* The search continued though as I knew there was more. In the Kingdom, seekers always find. Matthew 7:7 (NKJV) says, *"Ask, and it will be given to you; seek, and you will find…."* I was asking and seeking God. I was asking God to confirm to me in His Word and what He was saying to me. All the while, I continued to see 1111 *everywhere*!

John 11:11 Marked Me

Then, God said "John 11:11" to both my husband and me at the same time. At the time, I had no idea what that Scripture said, so I quickly opened my Bible and read it—I couldn't contain my excitement:

> *After he had said this, he [Jesus] went on to tell them, "Our friend Lazarus has fallen asleep; but I am going there to wake him up"* (John 11:11 NIV).

This story is about Jesus, resurrection life and awakening! Jesus spoke to His dead friend Lazarus, and he came back to life. I knew God was saying, "It's time to wake up." John 11:11 has since marked my life and ministry. This one prophetic word from God, through simple numbers, has imparted wild faith for revival and resurrection power. Every fiber of my being came alive as I read John 11:11. The numbers 1111 became a signpost, pointing to Jesus who is our resurrection, and speaking to me about revival, and saying "time to wake-up." Resurrection power is still available to call the dead places in our lives, families and nations back to life. God was reminding me, I'm the God of Lazarus still!

Every time I saw 1111 from then on, I knew God was reiterating the message, "Wake up!" It's a season of awakening. Call the dead things back to life. Decree to Lazarus situations in the grave to *"Come forth"* (John 11:43 NKJV). Speak over medical situations, families, cities, nations and prophetic destinies in the grave to "Come forth!" This became a deeply personal message of faith for me, as there were areas in my body that needed to come back to life. And it was also a confirming word to my husband and me to keep decreeing revival in the nations.

Later, God added more detail, but John 11:11 has become a life message of faith for revival and resurrection power. We minister this message all around the world.

Let me encourage you that many who see 1111 in particular are being led to Jesus through this unusual, but actually very common, way God is speaking—and not just Christians.

I spoke with a pastor of a large church recently who had been seeing 1111 for years and had been seeking its meaning. As he was pressing in for revival and souls, he was filled with such fire as I spoke John 11:11 over him and decreed an army of people marked by the power of speaking for Lazarus-style comebacks to those who needed salvation and restoration of their promises. Faith arose in him for revival in his people and city,

I also spoke to a young dad who was very often seeing 11:11 and sadly thought it was the time he would die, as he had read something about this on the Internet. He was not walking with God, but knew that he knew he was "seeing 1111." As I shared what God was saying and that it was his own personal wake-up call from God to come back to the Lord, the man's heart softened as he realized God was personally calling him to return to his heavenly Father's heart. This is also a great example of why the Internet needs godly content explaining this phenomena. Thousands and thousands of unbelievers are looking for the answer to what it means that they are suddenly being chased down by seeing the same number over and over. God is getting their attention, that's for sure.

While I have many minister friends who are fluent in the Hebrew numerical meaning of numbers in the Bible—and I love reading their books and learning from them—this was not my journey of discovering what these numbers meant. For me, it's been about childlike hunger to work out what I was seeing, and the joy of discovery in the search.

Even though I now know a little about studying the meaning of the Hebrew root and biblical meaning of numbers throughout the Scriptures, to be completely honest, when I first started seeing numbers, I didn't even know there was a Hebrew root! All I knew was God is real; He speaks, and I was hungry to know what He was saying to me. The simplicity of asking God what He is saying and recognizing His voice through seeing numbers—or in any other circumstance you need wisdom—is what I want to impart to you through sharing this truth, this hope! All believers are qualified to understand God's prophetic voice if we are filled with the Holy Spirit— even if how He is speaking to us is unusual.

TO BE CLEAR, I DO NOT ENDORSE NUMEROLOGY.

As mentioned at the beginning of this chapter, numerology in any form is not from God. I'm laboring this point so my stand is clear on the subject.

Just as God speaks, so does satan and demons, and he uses numerology as a tool to speak lies to people. They might get a message from numerology, but it won't be from God. It also won't bring peace or lead to God. It will instead consume them with fear for their future. I know that many people have searched in dark places for the meaning of life and to explain what they see. Googling for what seeing numbers means will, in most cases, lead people to sites full of New Age, deceptive, anti-God prophesies. I'm so glad that there is increasingly more biblical information on how God is using this fun way to lead people to Jesus.

There is NO power in numbers in and of themselves. The numbers are merely a sign pointing to God Almighty. When God communicates to us through numbers, or any form of speaking to us, it always leads us to greater connection to Jesus and His Word. I am talking about seeing and encountering certain numbers with such regularity that at some point it becomes obvious that God is trying to say something, and then we ask Him for wisdom. This may have happened to you, and let me encourage you that it's God! He loves you and He's talking to you.

When random people suddenly started asking me what seeing different numbers meant, I realized that people everywhere, in church and out of church, were experiencing this phenomenon and needed a biblical, godly, spiritual answer to what they were experiencing.

WHAT IS ONLINE GRIEVES ME.

I discovered people worldwide were seeing numbers, 1111 in particular. In fact, entire communities were established around what this meant. None of what I found online at the time was Jesus focused or biblically sound. Some sites were telling people that it was the time of their death, or spiritual nirvana moment that excluded Jesus, or leading people into demonic, fear-inducing words over their life. It was dark and lacked God's voice. Too many people I met were seeing numbers regularly and were unsure if it was truly God speaking to them—and this grieved me deeply.

I Had to Share What I Knew

I eventually sat down and wrote a small guide revealing the basics of what God had shown me about repetitively seeing numbers, to help those on a similar journey find God's voice and wisdom. I was compelled to provide a biblical, God-fearing guide that pointed people to Jesus.

I remember the day when I was writing it out with a healthy sense of fear of the Lord, as I was aware that I had not heard other ministries talk about this topic. I felt the weight of stepping into new territory and ensuring that I was sharing biblical wisdom from God. The article itself was written quickly; it was a message I had carried and prayed into for years. I also remember the moment I published it on our ministry website. I prayed for a long time as I was unsure what the reaction would be and knew some would not understand. It took a lot of courage at the time, but I finally published it online.

That one little blog post quickly took on a life of its own and soon there were upward of 20,000 hits a month and messages from all around the world, even until this day. I realized that the journey God had taken my husband and I on was a very common journey for thousands of others.

Through receiving these messages, we discovered that not only Christians are seeing numbers and seeking answers, but unbelievers. It's become very clear to me that the King's prophetic voice is speaking through using the repetition of numbers to people around the globe of every background and belief framework. God is using this means of communication as a knock, knock, knock, sparking curiosity and leading people to Himself.

What I initially thought was just a personal experience was actually a global phenomenon. God was, and is busy cutting through the noise of the world and grabbing the attention of many. What excites me the most is that people who don't know Jesus are being led by God's most wonderful, prophetic, and uniquely creative voice into connection and relationship with Him.

Who would have thought that seeing simple numbers over and over such as 1111 and 1234 could do such a thing? Nothing is impossible for our King Jesus who is very good at speaking every person's language.

Let me encourage you, if this is a way God is speaking to you, you're not going crazy and you're not imagining it. God captured your attention for a reason. If He keeps saying the same number over and over in different ways, then He really wants you to know the message of what it means. God is reiterating the same message because He knows you will need to hold on to it in the season to come. He is speaking truth and a personal prophetic word to your spirit.

EVERYONE WANTS A PERSONAL MESSAGE FROM GOD.

I've heard people say, "I'd love to get a text or personal, real-time message from God," and I often smile, as mostly people are seeing numbers on their phones—you may even have your phone full of screenshots of numbers you keep seeing! Isn't it just like God to use simple, everyday occurrences to send us a personal message.

As with any way God speaks, it's personal and specific. It's the same when His prophetic voice is showing you the same number repetitiously as it is when He's speaking to you through a dream or Bible verse you keep thinking of. And so I encourage you to ask God for wisdom to understand His messages.

While there are similarities in what God is saying, He may show you something different. The important thing with any prophetic word is to ask God for the interpretation, and remember He will never violate His Word.

What About Other Numbers?

I want to mention 911 in particular because many are seeing that number and it often makes people fearful, especially those in the United States. Remember, *"God has not given us a spirit of fear"* (2 Timothy 1:7 NKJV), and so evict fear and pray with peace and urgency. When I see 911, it means an urgent call to prayer. It carries with it an urgency in the spirit to intercede and to ask God to *"Command His angels concerning you to guard you in all your ways"* (Psalm 91:11 (NIV). It equally speaks of angelic protection.

Amos 9:11 (NLT) also speaks of restoration, repair and rebuilding and so I factor this into my prayers, decreeing restoration of God's purpose, promotion and prophetic destiny: *"In that day I will restore the fallen house of David. I will repair its damaged walls. From the ruins I will rebuild it and restore its former glory."*

As mentioned, many see different number sequences, in varying seasons. Some of the most common include 2222, 333, 888, 414, 444, 818, 777, 737, and 555. The combinations are many and personal; though as explained, there are often similarities in what the Lord is communicating.

My Caution for You Moving Forward

Discerning and seeking the meaning of God's prophetic voice through seeing numbers is not a formula; it's always first about relationship with God. Seeking God personally for what He is saying to you is paramount. He may give you a different meaning or verse to lean into, so seek the Holy Spirit and allow God's prophetic voice to prophesy to you. I bless you as you explore this fun and creative way God speaks.

Visit our website at www.pouritout.org and go to the blog section to read the original article called "What does 1111, 2222, 333, 911, 747 and other numbers mean?" I update this article regularly as God continues to give me insight, and I hope it helps stir you to hear what God is saying to you through numbers.

Mentoring Moment with the King

- Has God spoken to you through seeing repetitive number sequences? If so, what numbers and what do they say to you?

- Has the message of a number, or prophetic symbol, shifted and changed in different seasons?

- Has God ever chased you down with something to get your attention? How have you processed His pursuit of you?

- Take a moment and meditate on John 11:11, then turn it into a prayer for your circumstances, family, and nation.

- Are there grave clothes in your life that need to be discarded? Take a moment with the Lord and discard the unnecessary and unhelpful thoughts, habits, and things.

- What does Lazarus come-back faith look like for you in this season?

Activation Prayer

King Jesus, You are the God of resurrection power. I ask You to stir bold faith for resurrection power to call forth promises that are in the tomb. Stir me to believe for restoration and redemption of what the enemy has stolen from me. Lord, help me to never be satisfied with less than what the Bible says is available to me. Fill me with courage to push past comfortable faith and awaken costly faith. I ask for resurrection life and hope to surge through my body and awaken my first love for You, Jesus. Amen.

Practical Guide

The following is the practical guide I wrote that will help you discover what God is saying to you through the number sequence you are seeing, which can also be found on our website: www.pouritout.org.

It's not hard to translate the King's prophetic voice. The following questions and prompts will help you work out for yourself what the numbers you are seeing mean to you. Incidentally, these tips help with more than just seeing numbers—they will help you process any encounter for which you are seeking God's wisdom.

There are no right or wrong answers—these prompts help you begin the process of deciphering and turning mystery to message.

1. What is the number sequence you are seeing? Record it.

2. Thank God for this way He's speaking to you. Thankfulness opens doors to more understanding.

   Pray, for example: *Jesus, thank You for giving me wisdom when I ask You for it. I am asking You to show me what _____ means when I keep seeing it and what You are saying to me. Thank You for loving my curious heart and I wait on You for wisdom. Thank You, God, that You hear my voice, and I trust that You will bring further understanding to me. I also thank You, God, that You love me deeply and You are adding wisdom to me with tender kindness and I can expect You to speak to me with love. I do not need to fear Your voice or Your answers to my questions. I love growing in hearing Your prophetic voice, Lord. Amen.*

Now, enjoy processing the next few questions.

Tip 1: Don't write a thesis to answer these questions. The purpose of these questions is to prompt creative thinking; often God is answering or speaking to areas of your life for which you have already been seeking wisdom. You may be feeling stretched to grow in something, and God is giving you words of encouragement through what you are seeing. Often, seeing numbers is just the start of an ongoing conversation with God.

3. Take note of when you first started to see this number, and then ask and answer the following questions:

    *   When did I first see this number?

    *   Does this number mean anything to me personally already? For example, is it a birth date or street address, etc.

    *   Does this number remind me of any previous dreams or encounters I've had, or remind me of anything God is already bringing to my attention?

    *   When I see this number, does it consistently happen at a certain time, circumstance, or situation? If so, does this mean anything to me?

    *   What is going on in my season and situation?

    *   Was I praying or talking about anything in particular when I saw this number?

    *   Are there any common circumstances to when or how I see this number?

    *   Do I have a sense already what it could mean?

    *   If you saw the number in a dream or vision, what was going on in the dream and does the theme of the dream give you any context for what God is saying to you?

4. Ask God what He is saying to you and write down anything you hear. Then wait for God to add further wisdom or confirm what He's speaking to you about. (Don't be a perfectionist. Give yourself freedom to simply write your thoughts and evaluate them later.)

5. Is there a Bible verse that God is showing you that speaks directly to what He is saying and revealing to your heart? Often there is a Bible verse that correlates to the number you are seeing, but that is not always the case. God may highlight a Bible story, the Hebrew meaning of the number, or something personal the numbers mean to you. Remember, God will never say anything that violates or contradicts the Bible. He also loves to confirm His heart to us through the Bible.

6. What other things is God talking to you about lately? How would you describe your season? What are the general areas of growth God is stretching in you? What are the general areas of breakthrough you are pressing into? What general things are you believing for right now? What is on your heart lately? Is there something you know God is highlighting to you or has been stretching you in recently?

7. What are your main discoveries so far about this number sequence you are seeing? In one phrase or Bible verse, what does this number

say to you? (Remember it's okay if all the number is saying right now is, "You're seen and loved.")

Keep all your thoughts together in one place and keep track of what God says to you about this number, so you don't forget little things God drops into your heart at different times. I've found God often adds to the revelation rather than giving it all to you at one time.

Tip 2: After you have received some understanding…next time you see this number, thank God for what He is saying to you and receive it as a tender, personal message of hope and wisdom into your circumstances, heart, and life. Thank God specifically that this is what He is releasing into your life. If there's an invitation to pray or believe for extension of faith that comes with the meaning, take time to pray and receive fully what God is saying to you. Smile when you see the number—God sees you and loves you.

NOTE: For more information on numbers, please refer to Number Sequence Prophetic Meaning Guide

12

PAY ATTENTION TO PROPHETIC SYMBOLISM

Prophetic symbolism is a common way God speaks to us. Because it's sometimes perplexing, I want to mention a few prophetic symbols specifically to give you simple tools for understanding what God is saying, and why it's important to pay attention to prophetic symbolism. God is speaking through the supernatural and the natural as He highlights symbols and encounters and speaks into our lives.

Some of the more common ways God speaks prophetic messages:

- Repetitious number sequences (discussed in Chapter 11)
- Prophetic symbolism through signs and wonders
- Dreams and visions
- Angelic visitations and glory realm encounters
- Creative miracles and nature symbolism

The following are examples and mentoring keys to hearing God speak through prophetic symbolism:

Prophetic Symbolism Through Signs and Wonders

The importance of signs is not about the sign itself, it's about where it points. Specifically, I mean when God continually highlights something symbolizing a message to you, He is pointing you ultimately to Himself, the Message Giver. For instance, God may bring your attention to almonds (He's done that to us). You don't know what it means, but after a while, you most certainly know that God is getting your attention. The same process as for all other prophetic interpretation applies—evaluate, interpret, and apply.

Mostly what is needed in recognizing God's voice through symbolism is a hungry heart to search out what God is saying.

Almonds

Recently on a plane trip, my husband experienced a whole almond creative miracle. He had finished eating a pack of almonds and put the packet in the seat back pocket in front of him. When he reached in later to pull out the empty packet for the trash, he pulled out not only the empty packet, but also an entirely new packet of the same almonds. Yes, it was wild. At the time, we were making an important, urgent decision and it confirmed we needed to go to a certain place, and it spoke to us of multiplication for all we needed.

We knew there was more, though, because we saw almonds almost everywhere for that season. The next week as my husband unpacked a towel from his briefcase in a hotel room, there was an almond folded into the middle of the towel. Now God really had our attention.

Our daughter had a dream about almonds, and we started getting words about almonds. Earlier, I had a dream about receiving a "rod" in the mail (yes, random) and then months later, a well-known traveling minister preached on "the rod." Then later when he heard I had a dream about a rod, he ordered a rod with our prophetic word for the season inscribed on it, and sent it to our house. It was an old-style Aaron's rod engraved with our names and prophetic word. We knew the Bible talked about Aaron's rod that blossomed, but we were still asking God what He was saying to us. This game of "hide and seek" with the Lord of constant searching out a matter went on for months. We read the Bible about almonds and researched the topic, but for quite a while, nothing really hit us. Then one day as we read the Bible, God highlighted how almonds represent *awakening*—this resonated. The story continues to unfold, and it has been a joy from God confirming prophetic direction to us through the thrill of discovery.

Elephants and Re-digging Wells

God started highlighting elephants to me years ago. Eventually, after research and dreams and seeing them so very often, I knew God was using this symbolism to speak to me. I read and studied and watched countless videos of elephants in the wild. God highlighted in particular how elephants had an ability to "hear" through their feet. Among other things, they could sense the water under the ground in dry river beds where water used to flow, which helped them know where to dig (by stomping) for water.

I knew God was talking to me about re-digging the wells of revival, especially in places where water had flowed before, and that He was raising up a generation of mighty "elephants" who would stomp and dig and not give up until the wells of revival flowed again! This became a seasonal message with so much prophetic revelation for me—and it started with seeing elephants repeatedly and asking God what He was saying. Research what you're seeing and God will lead you until you understand the prophetic symbolism.

Amazingly, while as a family we were ministering in South Africa, we visited Kruger National Park (a wildlife reserve) and saw with our own eyes elephants stomping on the ground to dig up water. I was able to film this prophetic word while elephants were in the background "re-digging the wells"!

Feathers

While in South Africa, we saw God move mightily. Night after night, we saw a move of God in nightly meetings with many saved and healed. My husband was asked to speak at a public school, not a Christian school. (You can read the full story in his book, *When God Breaks In*.) He was given only 15 minutes to speak at this very prestigious school, very formal and "proper," and certainly not a place where the gospel would normally be preached.

When we arrived, we had some time alone as a family with our daughter in the school assembly hall, it was very imposing. Pictures of past students lined the walls who had become the nation's sporting heroes, politicians, and leading influencers.

We simply prayed and asked God for boldness and to speak through Ben that day.

As we prayed, a white feather manifested in front of our eyes and started floating to the ground. It was about two inches long. We watched it suddenly appear and then Ben grabbed it as we prayed. We immediately knew harvest angels were there with us. We thanked God for sending His angels. In prayer we called in souls and prayed for a move of God.

What happened next I will never, ever forget.

Ben boldly preached the gospel that day and closed with an altar call to an entire school of boys. When he asked those who wanted to say yes to Jesus to stand, we watched 1,000 boys stand up and give their lives to Jesus. With the exception of maybe a dozen in the room, an entire school received salvation that day! Surely God had sent angels with us. Not only that, the school principal stood with his students and was saved that day too. We cried a lot of joyful tears.

That feather was a sign that day—a sign of harvest angels in the room. My husband was sent there to preach the gospel to a school full of kids who needed God and He would have done it with or without seeing that feather; but seeing it was a gift from the Lord. That feather was a sign that prophesied souls redeemed! Be bold. Preach the Word, and pay attention when God is speaking, even through symbols that encourage us.

Hearing Fire Alarms

We have experienced strange "adventures" with fire alarms. My husband and I were recently ministering in the Smoky

Mountains in Tennessee. The first morning we were in our hotel, we were awakened very early by a fire alarm (of course I laughed, as it was the Smoky Mountains). It was a false alarm, but it happened again the next day. God brought to my attention a time years ago when we went through a season of repeatedly hearing fire alarms everywhere. He was talking to us about needing to burn for Him. It again felt prophetic, but I didn't know yet what God was saying, other than the obvious prophetic meanings.

Over the next few weeks, we often heard fire alarms. Our first night back home after our trip to the Smoky Mountains, I woke up around 2 a.m. and a firetruck was outside our house and firefighters were walking up and down our street, seemingly looking for a fire. I watched them for a few minutes, and then they got in the truck and left. Then twice in a row, we went to our church building and the fire alarm sounded. Later that week, the smoke alarm at our home randomly blared for no reason. Even when shopping, fire alarms would randomly sound. I woke up one night and smelled smoke, walked around the house looking for a fire, and nothing. The next night our smoke alarm randomly went off in the night again. This was going on over and over. We traveled away from home and the first night in the hotel, you guessed it, the fire alarm went off. This happened three times that night. As we went out for coffee the next day, a firetruck was parked in front of our car and firefighters were walking around in the hotel foyer. I *knew* God had a word for me.

Take note, prophetic friend, when something keeps happening that isn't usual, God is likely speaking!

After much prayer and recognizing that God was speaking, I heard the Holy Spirit speak to me in His inner audible voice, "Jodie, in a fire, souls matter!" And boom, I knew what God was saying to me: "SOUL! SOULS! SOULS! Saving souls is urgent right now. Focus on souls. Burn and release the fire and set people ablaze for revival and saving souls."

Where we were mistering when God said this was in a region in the United States that was currently experiencing fierce push back with legislation against the church meeting together, and there was a very heavy atmosphere of intimidation. As we ministered, we actively preached the gospel to the atmosphere as much as to the room. Despite the atmosphere, we preached the gospel to smash the intimidation, and go for souls as we knew God was saying, "SOULS! SOULS! SOULS!" Many salvations took place, healings, and spontaneous baptisms and deliverances. As it was a small town, we could keep track of how many were saved in that week—5 percent of the town's population! God's work there was extraordinary! His presence left a lasting and increasing impact on the town and us.

We preach the gospel everywhere we go; but in this place, we pushed back with fierce determination because the King's prophetic voice through a simple fire alarm was making His heart very clear. What matters in a fire? SOULS!

Signs matter. Most definitely souls matter. The King's prophetic voice matters. When God is speaking to us, even through prophetic symbolism or signs and wonders, it matters! Pay attention to signs and wonders.

Keys for understanding signs:

- First, recognize when God is highlighting something to you and take note.

- It might be "strange," but hold it in your heart until God says more.

- Research whatever repeatedly happens as God may be releasing a message to you; look for anything God breathes life on while you research.

- Take notice of where you are and what you are doing when God shows you a sign, as it may be significant.

- Ask God for wisdom, a Bible verse, or to confirm what He's saying.

- Don't overlook the simplest of messages, and let yourself have fun as you hear God communicating with you—no matter how "strange" or "unusual" it may seem.

Dreams and Visions

Dreams, visions and "flash visions," as I call them—when something drops in front of you—are somewhat "normal" in many people's lives. But when talking about trances and open-eye visions (that appear real), these expressions of the prophetic voice of God can be a bit less common and intimidating for people to understand and accept if they have not experienced this themselves.

Keep in mind that the Bible is full of dreams and visions, even profound dreams that saved people lives, including Jesus' life (Matthew 2:13). Peter saw an open-eye vision that changed his understanding of who could receive salvation (Acts 10:9-16). Actually, the Bible says Peter was in a trance, and it told him that Gentiles are included in salvation. That's big, and it came from a trance while he was praying. This encourages us to pay attention to our dreams, as they can give highly important directives or information about the future.

Koalas

I had simple dream of koalas playing in the desert that gave directional wisdom. It was such a fun, happy dream full of joy. I saw in the dream my daughter Keely and our spiritual daughter Lauren who lives with us, and both of them were laughing and happy.

Koalas are Australian, obviously, and at the time I thought the dream was just a word that even in wilderness times, God was bringing us fun and provision.

But remember, there are often layers to His prophetic voice.

Later, God started talking to us about moving to Arizona, a literal desert. The move was sudden, as God shifts often are. I had no idea at the time of the dream that we would be moving to the desert!

As we were seeking confirmation, God reminded me of my dream. This dream was one of many ways God used to help confirm our direction, and that it would be a good move for our family. I'm always amazed at the care and kindness of God. He cares about our families and wants us to know He cares about their hearts. The King's prophetic voice speaks and confirms through dreams, even the direction we should go.

My Life-Saving Dream

I had been in and out of the hospital and was at home recovering from a life-saving operation—except I wasn't recovering, I was getting worse. More tests and appointments found nothing wrong and no other need for surgery right then. Again I was told it would take time to recover. But pain and raging fevers remained. We were praying for healing and wisdom.

Then I had a simple dream. I saw in my dream a fiery, small red track, similar to a railroad track. It was glowing as if on fire. That was it. I woke up right away and I knew immediately that the "fiery track" symbolized a small and hidden "tract" of infection in my intestines that had not been found. I promptly went back to the doctor and graciously explained I believed there was a tract of infection remaining. After much discussion, another exploratory operation was cautiously agreed to, as I was still weak from the previous surgery, but all agreed that something was wrong.

The surgeon "searched and looked extensively" during the operation, but he couldn't find anything wrong in my intestinal tract. Then, the surgeon told us later, all of a sudden he saw a flash of light inside my body. So he looked where the light flashed, and in that exact spot is where he found a tiny tract of infection. Wow. God lit up exactly where the surgeon needed to look. Thank You, Jesus.

Dreams are "movies from Heaven," which is one way of thinking about them, and certainly a way God speaks to us, so it's imperative we pay attention.

My Waikiki Beach Dream

A decade ago, I had a movie-type dream. In part of the dream I was standing on Waikiki Beach in Hawaii. I had never been to Hawaii, but the dream felt very real. I could describe exactly what it looked like, smelled like, felt like—just as if I was watching a movie that came to life.

At the time, I was in the hospital facing life-threatening circumstances. I was in extreme pain, unable to walk, eat, and barely swallow water. I knew I had to have fierce faith in God, especially because the doctors had said there was no medical hope other than to remove my entire bowel and half my stomach and I would have to be fed through a tube for the rest of my life. Yeah, *that* was a moment of having to press into God and asking ourselves what we really believed.

Part of the story I often don't share is that about six months earlier, my husband had booked ridiculously cheap tickets to go to Hawaii for vacation to celebrate our daughter's birthday. After my hospitalization, we knew the trip scheduled for the following week would have to be cancelled. I kept being reminded, however, of the dream God had given me of standing on Waikiki Beach. Somehow I knew it was real and kept thinking, *I'm going there. I'm getting well. I will stand on that beach.*

Then an angel dropped into my hospital room with a clipboard showing all of God's promises written on it, and the angel started ticking them off one by one by one! Yes, another wow! My eyes were open, I watched it happen. By the next morning, I was already starting to recover and able to eat—a miracle! My healing took place; in part, from that angelic encounter. (I share more details about this miraculous healing in my book *The King's Decree.*)

I have shared some of this with you before, but it bears repeating now. I had been praying John 11:11 and was again repeatedly seeing 1111. Apart from having had revival break out in our church (yes, all this was happening at the same time), I was personally seeing 1111 in my dreams, on my phone, receipts, numerous times daily. My constant prayer and decree during this health crisis came from John 11:11 (NIV) when Jesus says, *"Our friend Lazarus has fallen asleep; but I am going there to wake him up."* And so I was decreeing, *"Lazarus, come forth"* over my bowel and medical situation (see John 11:43 NKJV). I was praying resurrection power to be manifested in my body.

A doctor I had never seen before or after came into my hospital room the day after the angelic encounter and discharged me! Yes, discharged. The day before, they had said there was no medical hope! The next day, I was discharged. Guess what the doctor' name is who discharged me? Dr. Lazarus! You can't make this stuff up!

After returning home, I attended church that night, as the Pineapple Revival was still going strong, and I could hardly stand up or walk, but I praised my face off thanking God for all He had begun and would complete in me. My promises were yes and amen. So are yours, friend.

So back to Waikiki. We hadn't cancelled the flights that were booked for only two days later. We decided that God had done so much—so many signs, wonders, miracles and even dreams that spoke of His promises to me—that I was definitely going on that trip! Two days later, our family boarded a plane and flew to Hawaii. I want to be real, it took faith. I was still very weak, but I also knew God had saved my life.

When we arrived at the hotel, we were given an upgrade to a room with a beach view (thank You, Jesus). When I walked into the room and looked out the window, I was staring at the exact view I had seen in my dream! I'm crying writing this. I had seen this beach, and this moment. God had gone ahead of me and laid treasure to help increase my faith for the fight of my life. He's so good.

As you can imagine, I looked at Ben and said, "Get me down to that beach!" The walk wasn't easy because the muscles in my legs had been eaten away and needed to be restored. My legs struggled to support my weight, especially after the long flight. But Ben helped me to the beach, and I stood on the sand. We cried and thanked Jesus. As I looked around again at the scene, I knew I'd been there before. The beach and the surroundings were exactly what I had seen and where I had stood over a decade before in my dream.

Let me be clear, this story involves seeing numbers, 1111 to be precise, having a dream where I felt like I had actually been there over a decade earlier, an open-eye vision of an angel, and a doctor whose name was wildly prophetically symbolic. Some may say that signs and supernatural visions are not important in the Christian life. I say they were used to save my life! Thank You, God, for speaking.

Friend, dreams matter. Prophetic symbolism matters. Supernatural signs matter. The King's prophetic voice matters.

Our God speaks, and hearing Him just may be more important than we think.

Keys for interpreting dreams:

1. Record your dream, trance, or vision, as it's often for a time years away.

2. Look for the main theme. Dreams often have multiple small details that can indeed hold important insight. However, don't become so bogged down in the details that you miss the main message.

3. Immediately interpret what you do know.

4. Start keeping track of your own personal dream language. If you keep having dreams about tsunami waves or helicopters or fishing poles, keep your own personal dream code. This may help you identify similar meaning in other dreams.

5. If you consistently have nightmares or tormenting dreams, this indicates a need for prayer to break off interference from the demonic realm in the night hours. If you need to, pray the following: "Jesus, I speak a cleansing and purifying over my seer, prophetic gifting and dream life. I break off all demonic, dark interference and rebuke any assignment of the enemy to interfere with my dreams by bringing fear, torment, or dark visions in Jesus' name. I repent of and renounce any involvement in

occultic, demonic, anti-Jesus, and New Age practices that have given access to the enemy, (name them to God), and I receive Your forgiveness. I ask You to wash me clean and fill me afresh with Your Spirit. I receive a purifying of my spiritual eyes and dream life now in the name of Jesus. I call dreams from God's glory realm, righteous revelation in the night hours, and angelic encounters in the day hours. I receive all You have for me in Jesus' name, amen."

6. Interpretation of dreams is a gift. Often when I interpret dreams, I get a download. I pray until something drops, and I have sudden insight into what a prophetic dream means. At times I sit and just interpret dreams, layer by layer; but more often than not, an interpretation will come from prayer. I encourage you to simply ask God for wisdom and insight, and pray expecting revelation to come. I don't always receive revelation; but as I've stewarded this gift, understanding has increased.

The list isn't an exhaustive teaching on interpreting dreams, but it highlights the most important keys that will help you hear and recognize God's prophetic voice.

Angelic Visitations and Supernatural Glory Realm Encounters

As we've discussed, angelic visitations are normal occurrences reported throughout the Bible—and continue today. An angelic encounter was used by God in our ministry to give us a mandate from Zechariah 4 to pour out the oil of God's presence in the nations. When we see angels or dream of angels, ask the important question: Is the angel pointing me to Jesus? Angelic visitations from God will always point to Jesus and never violate the Bible. Just as Jesus' birth was announced by angels, in times of transition and birthing new things in the Lord, angelic activity is increased.

As with dreams and prophetic symbolism, what God is saying through the angelic visitation in a dream, vision, or with eyes open is important—do not miss what God is releasing and imparting to you.

Some people "see" angelic activity, as when particular angels are released with ministry assignments from Heaven to impart on earth. For instance, I saw a flash vision of angels in California ready to sign up whoever was willing to pay a "costly yes" for the harvest and revival. These angels were recording responses and imparting courage for the new season of harvest and revival, despite the cost, despite persecution. These angels were partnering with God's people in the harvest. Angels are sent to minister and serve God's people. *"Are not all angels ministering spirits sent to serve those who will inherit salvation?"* (Hebrews 1:14 NIV).

Sometimes the encounter may not involve actually seeing an angel, but an angelic presence is felt or seen, but it is most definitely a glory realm encounter. For instance, being "caught up" in an atmosphere of glory, having a sudden vision or awareness of Heaven, or encountering something supernatural from the glory realm. In these encounters sometimes the supernatural is superimposed over the natural realm, or you can have a vision of something supernatural and are aware it's symbolic of what God is releasing in the natural. For instance, seeing angels holding "leaves" and knowing they are symbolic of healing (see Revelation 22:2 NIV).

It can be as simple as an impartation and upgrade or a mandate for a new season. The key is to apply and receive in your life what the angelic or glory realm encounter is releasing.

Creation Miracles and Nature Symbolism

> *For since the creation of the world God's invisible qualities—his eternal power and divine nature—have been clearly seen, being understood from what has been made, so that people are without excuse* (Romans 1:20 NIV).

All Creation Prophesies—Including "This Bird"

Creation itself testifies about God's glory and goodness. Sometimes that testifying looks like creation prophesying. Let me explain. No doubt you have experienced when nature comes alive and seems to speak directly to you, such as watching a sunrise or seeing a rainbow in a needed moment. I have also witnessed a bird that flew in during a meeting and "trumpeted" a song for about twenty minutes. It actually sounded like a trumpet. At first the sound was annoying, but after about ten minutes I (and many others) became aware that the bird was releasing breakthrough. The atmosphere literally started to shift from heavy to joyful, and everyone sensed it. It was one of those moments when creation testified and prophesied—and those who had "ears to hear" heard.

Ladybug

Many have experienced the "anointed" love of a pet or when an animal has been used by the Lord to protect or warn someone. God uses His creation for the benefit of His family. Just recently a friend of mine, whose son was going through a really difficult time, went outside to pray for a breakthrough in a court case. She looked down, and right in front of her, God highlighted a ladybug. She knew God was showing her this ladybug as a prophetic symbol. In her words, "In the natural, ladybugs eat aphids that destroy plants and the harvest." This ladybug spoke to her a message of breakthrough coming from the Lord. Sure enough, that day miraculous breakthrough came in her son's court case. God ate up the "aphids" that were preventing the breakthrough harvest of promise.

Praying Mantis and Butterflies

Praying mantises have shown up in my home at significant times of warfare, and I knew God was using this creature as a sign to intercede. Equally, in a time of transition recently, every day for a few weeks, swarms of butterflies appeared in my backyard. I had literally just released a prophetic word about new beginnings and coming out of the cocoon, and the next morning God used butterflies as I prayed outside to prophesy to my heart. It went on for weeks, with butterflies even landing on the table beside my Bible and journal.

Hail and Ice

> ...*the Lord hurled large hailstones down on them, and more of them died from the hail than were killed by the swords of the Israelites* (Joshua 10:11 NIV).

I originally heard my friend Katie Souza preach on this verse in Joshua 10, using it to talk about God bringing the breakthrough. God won the battle for the Israelites; taking out the enemy by hurling hailstones down on them. Hail and ice have since become symbols of breakthrough to me.

On vacation in Florida one morning, I was walking on the beach specially decreeing Joshua 10:11 and speaking breakthrough over ongoing attacks on my health, calling down hail to smash the enemy. As I looked up, I smiled seeing that I was standing right in front of 10-foot sign with the word, "ICE"! Later that week as I was praying, it suddenly started to hail. There was no rain in the forecast, so I knew it was prophetically prophesying breakthrough to me. Huge hailstones started pelting down as I sat in my prayer room. Incredibly, the pain started to shift in my body, and within hours there was an incredible healing breakthrough. The ice was truly prophesying breakthrough as I decreed. This has happened again several times, at very specific moments.

Several times now as I have publicly prophesied "I hear the sound of heavy rain" (see 1 Kings 18:41) and prayed for revival, it has suddenly begun to rain—as in heavy rain! The rain itself seemed to prophesy revival outpouring!

You probably have had moments when you knew that you knew creation was testifying to you, and nature was prophesying to your heart. Take note when God highlights something in creation to you. Allow creation to testify of God's glory and prophesy God's word into your life. The point is, when the King's prophetic voice is speaking, we should pay attention.

GOD'S ABILITY TO SPEAK THROUGH PROPHETIC SYMBOLISM IS ENDLESS.

God speaks through prophetic symbolism in so many ways. Just as Jesus often spoke in parables, God loves to speak through prophetic symbolism that conveys a multilayered message to our hearts. God is the Ultimate Communicator and most Masterful Storyteller. Pay attention to the signs, symbolism, dreams, angels, nature miracles, and encounters that God gives you as the King is speaking to those who have "ears to hear and eyes to see" (see Proverbs 20:12 NIV).

Ears to hear and eyes to see—both are gifts from the Lord (Proverbs 20:12 NLT).

Mentoring Moment with the King

- Considering all the ways God's prophetic voice has interacted in your life, has there been a time God has spoken through the supernatural that changed your life?
- Can you identify times when God imparted new anointing or fresh courage through an encounter with creation, symbolism, or signs?

- What prophetic symbolism has God used in recent encounters that has spoken to you?

- As you look at an overview of how God has been speaking to you in the past season, what has He been preparing you for or stirring vision for?

- What is God encouraging you to boldly believe?

- How has God used prophetic symbolism or dreams to encourage you?

- What symbol does God use most in your life to speak to you lately?

- Can you sum up what God has been stirring in you through His prophetic voice in one sentence?

Activation Prayer

Lord Jesus, help me to pioneer with You. Grow my capacity to dream with You, God, and establish God dreams in my family and sphere of influence. Grow my capacity to believe all that You are releasing to me. Help me faithfully and obediently step forward with You into new promise and new depth of relationship with You. Would You stir me with anointed boldness to care more what You think of me, and less what people think of me. I ask for a healthy fear-of-the-Lord upgrade, to seek You first and courageously walk out my call and promises. Amen.

13

HELP! I'M STUCK IN PERPETUAL MYSTERY

W HEN GOD'S PROPHETIC VOICE IS MORE MYSTERY THAN message, it can be hugely frustrating. God will journey with us into the message He is giving us, but part of the process is trusting He is good; and while curiosity is a God-given gift, confusion does not come from Heaven.

I suggest you may have encounters with the King's prophetic voice quite commonly or have had seasons when the supernatural or symbolic nature of how God is speaking to you has been intense, mysterious, and seemed to spark more questions than answers. The ebbs and flows of experiencing encounters with the prophetic can be wonderful and challenging.

For instance, you may find yourself in a season of vivid dreams that come one after the other. And yet, you are unsure of what any of them mean and may be overwhelmed by the amount of revelation. I get it. There are times when experiencing the prophetic voice of the King is exciting, overwhelming, immeasurably wonderful, and almost frustrating and burdensome to evaluate.

WHEN THE WAVE RECEDES, PAUSE IN HIS PRESENCE.

Let me encourage you—this is normal. Times of increased (or decreased) revelation are part of the journey; as we progress from glory to glory, like wave after wave, revelation comes. When the wave recedes, pause in His presence and allow the Holy Spirit to lead you as you evaluate what He has said. It's important to learn the rhythm of the Kingdom, which I describe as wave after wave. It's constant, but the intensity is fluid, constantly changing.

> *Deep calls to deep in the roar of your waterfalls; all your waves and breakers have swept over me* (Psalm 42:7 NIV).

Selah

The Kingdom of God has a rhythm: there are times of intense revelation, warfare, and pressing in; and there are times of recalibration, application, rest, and preparing for the next set of waves. In the moments after a set of waves, it's important to "Selah"—pause in His presence and take in what He's saying. When the wave stops, breathe, look around for what's coming next, and evaluate what you just learned. If you ride the wave, you will now be in a new position, as the glory advances you. But between waves, rest in His presence and take this moment to seek the Lord for strength, refueling, and prophetic understanding.

When the revelation is coming, ride the wave. Record and take note what God is saying. Allow the Holy Spirit to wash over you, and know that the waves are not there to overwhelm you, but to move you forward. Don't over-process in the breaker waves, just ride the wave, and surrender to what God is releasing and doing in you.

When the waves of revelation subside, run to the secret place, process what God's saying, and pause in His presence for rejuvenation. Use these moments to recalibrate and renew, and prepare for the next wave with the added revelation from the last wave.

I understand this explanation oversimplifies the process; as in reality, there's a mix of wave motions happening every day. But there are definite moments when you can sense that you need to run or rest. Taking time to refocus and process what God is saying adds clarity of vision. There are definite moments when it's more about receiving than running, and other moments when it's doing what you know to do in the intensity of the season.

So, in times of increased revelation and when you receive more than you can process, the following tips will help:

1. Record (Journal)

Record what you experience without stressing over immediate interpretation. Recording can look like journaling, writing down dreams, jotting down a note of what you experienced and felt, and making a mental note that God is speaking. Write down what you initially know or sense. There may be very simple interpretations and you immediately have wisdom.

If you know there is more but you're not sure yet what God is fully saying, note what you *do* know, and turn what you don't know into a prayer

2. Research

There may be obvious research you can do to help interpret what you experienced. For instance, if you had an encounter about an owl and eagle, researching facts about owls and eagles will add prophetic insight. Or if you dreamt about a particular nation, you may want to research that nation and what is going on there right now. A particular verse or story in the Bible may immediately come to mind, and reading God's Word will, of course, add wisdom. But don't obsess; as you research, allow the breath of the Holy Spirit to highlight what He is drawing to your attention.

3. Don't Obsess or Stress

As you wait for more, trust God that understanding will be added to you—often revelation comes in waves. Sometimes even multiply layers of revelations come even years later, which is also why recording supernatural experiences is important for remembering what God was doing.

Simply ask God for wisdom. Then leave it. Don't obsess over the process. God will answer your request for wisdom in His timing. Keep seeking Him, that's the bigger key. When you keep seeking Him and His righteousness, everything (including the wisdom to know what God is saying to you) will be given to you!

The Divine Tension of Not Knowing Yet

Divine tension is the healthy urging in our spirit to understand what God is saying and this compels us to press in until we hear more, and the tension of resting in, and enjoying Jesus while we wait.

In the moments of increased revelation, ask yourself, *Am I obsessed with* Jesus *right now, or am I more obsessed with the rabbit hole of mystery?*

I say that cautiously, as I'm not in any way suggesting that passionate, frenzied, determined seeking of God for answers should be shamed. I'm saying this with love as someone who walks this journey daily with you. May our greatest obsession be Jesus.

There are always things we don't yet understand fully and we need prophetic insight for. We will not grow in our discernment of receiving prophetic insight for the unusual encounters we are receiving if the supernatural encounters and unusual experiences are taking up more bandwidth than seeking Jesus Himself. Being in God's presence simply to be in God's presence is the ultimate goal, and a fast track to growing wisdom and insight.

The Giver of wisdom is Jesus. He is wisdom. Seek Jesus and you will grow in wisdom. (See Proverbs 16:16; James 1:5; Proverbs 3:13; Proverbs 9:10.)

> THE FEAR OF THE LORD IS THE BEGINNING OF WISDOM, AND KNOWLEDGE OF THE HOLY ONE IS UNDERSTANDING (PROVERBS 9:10 NIV).

Evaluate and Apply

That said, friend, you can't evaluate an encounter without focusing on the encounter, so please don't hear what I'm not saying to you. God loves to speak to you in creative ways and loves watching you search out the interpretation. It's meant to be fun, relationship building, and faith expanding. Whatever you do, remember to enjoy this process.

1. Evaluate

Take what you know and evaluate the main themes and message. What do you know God is saying? Set aside what you don't know yet, and look for what you do know. If a particular part of an encounter, dream, or experience is evading your understanding, set it aside and allow the Holy Spirit to "hover over it" just like He hovered over the waters before He spoke creation into being. The hovering and percolating of the Spirit is part of the process.

2 Apply

This is likely the most important part of the process. Take what you know now and apply it to your life. That may look like a prayer directive to intercede for something. It may be passing on a word to someone or putting into practice the wisdom and strategy God has given you to help you practically navigate your circumstances. Applying what you know may look like taking action in an area of your life or giving you impartation for faith and courage that then requires stepping into God's promise. It may be increased understanding of who God is to you, which will impact your ongoing relationship in pragmatic ways with God and others. Applying what you know may look like recalibration, repentance, or even course correction. Or it may be reminding yourself of key truths and promises God has already said to you, and how much God loves you. Applying what you know may look like actively seeking God for the more He is stirring you into and breaking off complacency. But application is active, not passive. You will be blessed as you apply what the King's prophetic voice has been saying to you.

TRUTH BOMB—GOD ADDS NO SORROW TO HIS BLESSING.

The blessing of the Lord brings [true] riches, and He adds no sorrow to it [for it comes as a blessing from God] (Proverbs 10:22 Amplified).

This verse is a big one to grasp in your prophetic journey. When you hear God's prophetic voice as part of your "normal" experience with God, the enemy loves to try and turn what God has given you as a blessing, into a curse.

Let me explain. Having multiple dreams or supernatural experiences or noticing prophetic symbolism is a blessing. Hearing God is a blessing. Experiencing signs and wonders is a blessing. Hearing God and seeing visions even in unusual ways is a blessing. Encounters with Jesus are always a blessing.

The enemy wants to take what is good and try to reassign it as "not good." The enemy wants you to think a prophetic lifestyle is a burden and overwhelming, and wants you to feel as though you will never understand or enter breakthrough. In this way, the enemy tries to turn a gift in your life into a curse. If the enemy is trying to do this to you, you will make comments like, "I'm so exhausted from all the dreams (or revelation)," or "I keep having encounters but they seem to add more worry and confusion," and "What I see is heavy and weighs me down, I wish they would stop."

Mentoring Moment

If this resonates with you, I want to speak truth over you, friend, and encourage you to speak the following decree out loud:

> *The blessing of the Lord brings true riches, which includes His voice and how He speaks to me. God adds no sorrow to His favor for me; all God's ways come as a blessing from God to me. Therefore, where the enemy has come at me to turn my prophetic gift and how I hear God into anything less than a blessing in my life, I break this lie in Jesus' name. I evict the assignment of the enemy to entrap me in fear or perpetual confusion or anxiety about how I hear the King's prophetic voice. In Jesus' name, I receive peace, joy, and I call back the intended blessing that my unique friendship with God and the way I hear His voice brings to my life. I am blessed to hear God. I am blessed by what He adds to my life. I am blessed in all my ways as I seek the Lord. Thank You, Jesus, for blessing me. Amen.*

Enjoy the journey of hearing God, my friend. It's a blessing.

Breaking Perpetual Confusion

Another biggie for anyone who feels stuck in mystery and never arriving at the message, is the sense of perpetual confusion. While it's normal to have times of seeking understanding, living in a state of perpetual confusion over what God is saying to you is not God's intention, my prophetic friend. If the greatest emotion you feel in your process of hearing God is confusion, you must evict confusion in your life in Jesus' name. Mystery is not confusion. Seeking wisdom is not the same as confusion. The thrill of discovery is not confusion. Perpetual confusion is not your inheritance. Peace, wisdom, and a sound mind is your portion from the Lord. (See 2 Timothy 1:7; Isaiah 26:3.)

THE AUTHOR OF CONFUSION IS THE DEVIL.

If you have been plagued, tormented, or paralyzed by confusion, know that it is *not* from God. The hallmarks of perpetual confusion are fear, paralysis of making decisions to move forward, continual doubting if and what God is saying to you, foggy thinking, swirling thought processes, unending uncertainty, indecision, hesitation to stand on God's Word, and anxiety attached to hearing and understanding God, and constant lack of peace.

How sneaky and mean is the devil? He still says to God's children as he said to Eve, "Did God really say…?" The devil is invested in destroying your ability to hear the King's prophetic voice with clarity and confidence. Even more than that, the devil wants to steal your joy in hearing God, and enjoying His prophetic voice to you.

Mentoring Moment

Okay, let's smash this thing! Pray the following prayer with me, friend:

In Jesus' name, I bind and rebuke every assignment of confusion that wants to keep me from using my God-given birthright to speak to and hear my heavenly Father. Where confusion, lies, fear, and anxiety have come at me to steal clarity, peace, and ease of hearing the voice of God, I break these strongholds right now in Jesus' name. Every and any demonic assignment sent to interfere with my ability to hear God and enjoy friendship with King Jesus is evicted now in Jesus' name. I silence the voice of the enemy, and call back clarity, sharpness of hearing, and a sound mind. I call back childlike joy and the excitement of searching out a matter with my King. I call in new healthy pathways of thinking about hearing from You, Lord, and command all tormenting confusion to go from my life and mind now. I am surrounded by Your glory realm of revelation from Heaven, and I receive peace and wisdom as I seek You. I ask for impartation even now of fresh love for Your voice, Your word, and new clarity, discernment, and passion for understanding all You say to me. In Jesus' mighty name, amen.

Goof-Proof Yourself

I don't really like the term "goof-proof," but I use it because it helps explain the concept easily. I do not think that the supernatural is in any way goofy, but sometimes, sadly, we can come across goofy in our explanation of it. So please hear this with a smile.

There's some simple ways to "goof-proof" yourself and your delivery of the King's prophetic voice. Much of this wisdom I have already covered in this book, but it bears repeating.

I consider the following three keys plain simple wisdom, necessary as we journey in the supernatural expressions of God's voice.

1. Stay connected to the body.

It is so important to be connected and remain connected with the body of Christ—a community of Bible-believing believers. I recognize the season has given opportunity for this to happen in different ways, but the truth is we need each other. And those who are prophetic, especially if you are hearing God consistently in supernatural ways, need biblical community as a safeguard and a sounding board. Iron sharpens iron, the prophetic sharpens and fine-tunes the prophetic, and wise counsel adds needed input in our lives, especially as the day of His return is drawing near (see Hebrews 10:25). Whether it's online or in person, large or small, have a community that knows you, grows you, and speaks into your life. A healthy spiritual community also looks outward, to the harvest—Jesus burns for the lost.

> *Plans fail for lack of counsel, but with many advisers they succeed* (Proverbs 15:22 NIV).
>
> *And the spirits of the prophets are subject to the prophets* (1 Corinthians 14:32 NKJV).

And let us not neglect our meeting together, as some people do, but encourage one another, especially now that the day of his return is drawing near (Hebrews 10:25 NLT).

2. Make the message "plain" and simple to understand.

Then the Lord answered me and said: "Write the vision And make it plain on tablets, That he may run who reads it" (Habakkuk 2:2 NKJV).

This is one of those profoundly wise verses that gives such simple wisdom. It simply means, as you process the mystical and prophetic, translate what you have experienced into simple and plain language and concepts so that those who hear your word can actually understand it. Our job with the prophetic voice of the King is to help people hear God's message through the symbolic. Take some time and lean in with the Lord until you can make it practical. Of course I'm not suggesting that you despiritualize the supernatural. But I am saying the purpose of the prophetic is to inscribe it clearly so that others may easily understand and run with it.

3. Keep the main thing the main thing.

It's all about Jesus. The entire purpose of the King's prophetic voice is to lead you and others to Jesus. The point of the sign is not the sign itself—it's where the sign is pointing. The purpose of the encounter is not the encounter itself—it's where the encounter leads you. May it be to Jesus. Nothing is wrong with being in awe of what God does and says and having fun, as His ways are glorious. But let's remember to recalibrate our hearts and check if the main thing is truly the main thing in our lives.

Mentoring Moment with the King

- What does "deep calls to deep" mean to you?
- Are there any areas you feel God is growing to add skills to flourish or rid yourself of perpetual confusion?
- What practical things can you implement to help find "selah" moments?

Activation Prayer

Lord, help me to discern when the breakers are coming and it's time to ride the wave, and when it's time to rest in Your presence. Lord, I tell all confusion and fear to be removed from my journey of hearing You, and instead I receive peace and clarity of vision. Give me eagle-eye vision for the season ahead and confidence to take the next step. Break me out of paralysis of analysis, and instead enable me to boldly step into new territory with You. Amen.

Part Three

WHAT DOES ALL THIS MEAN FOR MY LIFE?

Here am I, and the children the Lord has given me. We are signs and symbols in Israel from the Lord Almighty, who dwells on Mount Zion (Isaiah 8:18 NIV).

14

THE INVITATION OF THE PROPHETIC ENCOUNTER

I say it often and I mean it—I'm ruined for the ordinary. God has shown me so much that it's my responsibility to take it, steward it, and give it away. As we pour it out, He pours more in. God has ruined you for the ordinary, so you will expect extraordinary.

Arise, for this matter is your responsibility. We also are with you. Be of good courage, and do it (Ezra 10:4 NKJV).

> YOU WILL BE RUINED FOR THE ORDINARY, SO EXPECT THE EXTRAORDINARY!

Invitations from the King's Prophetic Voice

Within the supernatural encounters of His voice, there are invitations. Accepting the Holy Spirit's invitation opens the door for the extraordinary in our future journey with God.

These invitations will activate you to go beyond simply having an encounter, to establishing a new normal in your life.

The following three invitations, when activated, will change your life.

1. *Choose to do whatever He tells you.*

As we recognize what God is saying and increasing our faith for, the responsibility increases to actually do *"Whatever He says to you, do it"* (John 2:5 NKJV).

This is not a season for procrastination; rather, it is a season to quickly do the things He is talking to us about through His prophetic voice. Acceleration is upon us, and increasingly so. Allowing the prophetic voice of the King to actually influence our lives is the key to accelerating into God's promises.

> THE SEASON IS VOLATILE, AND THE OPPORTUNITIES ARE UNPRECEDENTED.

Despite the wild adventure of hearing God, or perhaps even because of it, I am ruined for the ordinary. The season continues to be volatile, but the opportunities continue to be unprecedented.

For certain, there are doors of opportunity for revival and harvest for you that are open windows to exploit. The Bible says there are treasures to be found in darkness.

> *I will give you the treasures of darkness and hidden riches of secret places* (Isaiah 45:3 NKJV).

Stored up and reserved for God's people are hidden riches and treasures as you walk through a dark season, situations, and challenging times. If you are going to go through it, you may as well collect the treasure that has been hidden for you to find while passing through. Keep in mind that it is not hidden *from* you, but *for* you. And most definitely hidden from the enemy. This treasure is to be discovered by God's people, right in the middle of your darkest of days. That means there are revelations, divine solutions, and supernatural treasures reserved for now, for you.

Hearing His voice gives access to the road maps that unearth the treasures of darkness and hidden wealth of secret places. Ask the Lord to reveal what He has set aside for you in this season. Ask Him to open doors of opportunity in the difficult places. He has trained our ears to hear, and this is the season for double restoration. Expect increase despite the season. His voice is leading you to take advantage of the opportunities of the season—not get stuck in the challenges of the season.

The key is though, "Do whatever He tells you." This is an invitation. It's one thing to recognize the King's prophetic voice, it's another to translate it, and then another to do what He's saying.

Go over what you've been hearing from the Lord. What are the common themes? Is there anything you know you haven't done? Are there practical things you can put in place to do what He has been saying? Are there ways you can put processes in place to allow you to better follow through when God speaks? Is there a main theme to all God is growing you in through His voice? How can you steward that well right now? And remember grace in the process.

> ## YOUR FAITH IN THE KING'S PROPHETIC VOICE PULLS FUTURE BLESSINGS INTO YOUR CURRENT CIRCUMSTANCES.

Keep this in mind, friend. When Mary said, "Do whatever He tells you," it resulted in one of the most profound creative miracles in the Bible—water turned into wine. And this miracle signified a new season for Jesus and the church, as Mary's faith brought into the now what Jesus said was still for another time. When Jesus replied, *"My hour has not yet come,"* He allowed Mary's faith to bring future blessing forward into the now (John 2:4 NKJV).

When you step out in bold faith and do whatever He is telling you, it births the miraculous and calls forth even what is reserved for another season, into the now. Your faith in the King's prophetic voice pulls future blessing into your current circumstances. Come on, somebody! We need this. This is definitely an invitation you want to accept from the King.

So what now? Keep it simple—do whatever He tells you.

2. Choose fire, not fear.

Inevitably, there are moments when the encounter you have leads to a choice—I urge you to choose fire, not fear. Just as Moses chose to turn aside and hear the voice from the fiery burning bush, you too will have to choose to turn aside when the King is speaking. That's the invitation, to move on or to turn aside to the burning bush encounter God is inviting you into.

Fire is unpredictable. Fire can make some fearful, and yet others lean in. The invitation of the season is to lean in and hear the Voice from the fire, rejecting fear at its root. The Voice from the fire is the invitation to a generation right now that we can't afford to ignore.

TO HEAR THE VOICE FROM THE FIRE IS YOUR PERSONAL INVITATION OF THE HOUR.

One of the most amazing and saddest stories in the Bible is when the Israelites were gathered as a nation and stood around Mount Horeb, and the Lord descended on the mountain in fire, with the intention of communicating with the entire nation just as He did with Moses.

> *The Lord spoke to you face to face out of the fire on the mountain.* (At that time I stood between the Lord and you to declare to you the word of the Lord, because you were afraid of the fire and did not go up the mountain) (Deuteronomy 5:4-5 NIV).

God spoke to the whole nation, face to face from the fire. That means that His voice was heard and His presence was observable. Deuteronomy 5 makes it clear that His voice sounded like thunder, and from the midst of the darkness, blazing fire was seen. The booming voice of the Lord was physically heard by the whole nation at one time, as God invited

His people to draw near so He could talk to them face to face. Now *that's* an encounter with the King's prophetic voice!

But when the people heard the fierce, thundering, blaring sound of God's voice and saw the blazing, consuming fire of His glory, instead of running toward God, they put distance between themselves and God. They chose not to hear God's voice face to face; rather, they made Moses hear from God for them. An entire generation rejected God's voice because they didn't like how it sounded and looked. They chose fear instead of fire. The Bible tells us they "were afraid because of the fire." Basically, they rejected the King's prophetic voice!

> *When you heard the voice out of the darkness, while the mountain was ablaze with fire, all the leaders of your tribes and your elders came to me. And you said, "The Lord our God has shown us his glory and his majesty, and we have heard his voice from the fire. Today we have seen that a person can live even if God speaks with them. But now, why should we die? This great fire will consume us, and we will die if we hear the voice of the Lord our God any longer. For what mortal has ever heard the voice of the living God speaking out of fire, as we have, and survived? Go near and listen to all that the Lord our God says. Then tell us whatever the Lord our God tells you. We will listen and obey"* (Deuteronomy 5:23-27 NIV).

The same invitation to hear God's voice from the fire is being given to a generation right now. Will we choose the fire or fear? Will we choose to hear and see God as He is or choose to keep Him at arm's length and receive Him only in ways that are comfortable? Will we choose to hear the Voice from the fire or step backward because it sounds different from how we imagined?

THE KING'S PROPHETIC VOICE IS NOT TAME.

Indeed, the King's prophetic voice is not tame. It's not predictable, comfortable, or containable. He is the Lamb *and* the Lion. To be specific, He chose to come to a people, a whole nation, as a roaring, blazing fire—not a peaceful, campsite fire with marshmallows. He wanted a people who would courageously choose fire over fear. He wanted a people who would trust Him even where it was not comfortable. His Voice is still inviting us into this place of surrender. Encounters with the King's prophetic voice are not always tame. But the King is inviting us to know Him as the Lion *and* the Lamb.

SOMETIMES GOD TESTS OUR RESOLVE.

The King's prophetic voice is not always predictable, comfortable, or cozy. At times, God talks through His still small voice; at times He roars with fire that tests our resolve.

Listening to the voice of God requires a choice sometimes, such as when confronted with the fire on the mountain, the voice from within the blazing fire, the modern-day burning bush encounters that force us to choose which way we will go. Surrender sometimes costs—if not always costs. But the fire is only fearful when we choose not to surrender.

The prophetic voice of the King is sometimes soft and sometimes loud, sometimes He whispers peace, and sometimes He leads us beside still waters—but other times, He is fire and burns things up. The Israelites wanted a campfire with toasted marshmallows, and instead they got the God of thundering fierceness showing them there is no stronghold, no Goliath, and no city walls that are beyond the reach of God Almighty. We need this God in our lives.

Just like the Israelites, we have a choice. Comfortable or costly? Lean in or draw back? Fire or fear? I want His fire. I want the King's prophetic voice in my life regardless of how He chooses to speak. The invitation from the King's prophetic voice activates the extraordinary in our midst when we receive Him as not just the Lamb, but the Lion.

3. Choose to stay sharp.

There's equally an invitation from the King's prophetic voice right now to refocus, refine, and resharpen. God is returning to His people the cutting edge, where we've felt blunt and dry. We are the head and not the tail (see Deuteronomy 28:13), but to be that requires getting our cutting edge back.

I know there are moments in our lives when, if we take stock, we can feel the sharpness of other seasons evading us. The hunger in our hearts for more can be dampened by the circumstances that seem to speak louder.

I remember a trusted minister gave Ben and me a word many years ago that impacted deeply and caused honest reflection. She simply said (I'm summarizing from memory), "The Lord is so well pleased with your faith and the way you have followed His voice into uncharted waters. But the Lord would also say that the faith of the last season that produced all these incredible testimonies must be replicated again for a new season of testimonies. If you camp where you are, you will continue to have a vibrant ministry and God will bless it. People will hear your stories and be amazed and ministered to, but you will stop having new cutting-edge stories. Nobody will know, as your ministry will be blessed. But you will know that you lost something if you don't step out again on the waters like you did before."

Whoa. Yeah, OUCH. It was a word that changed our lives. I'm being vulnerable sharing it, but goodness, that word was the kindness of the Lord—it was a Lion not a Lamb word! We didn't feel any harshness from God. Rather, it was His grace. The Voice from the fire was inviting us to believe for more again, to push past resistance and not settle for comfortable.

PERPETUALLY STIR HUNGER FOR FRESH-AND-CURRENT IN YOUR PROPHETIC JOURNEY.

That word from God started a journey of stirring hunger *again* in us. It's the cry of my heart to perpetually stir hunger for the fresh and the current. I want a move of contagious revival fire in my midst and in my life. There is always more. In fact, during the Pineapple Revival, one of the things God said that impacted me the most was, "To you who has had more, there is still more!" That's a boom right there. To you who has had more, there is still more.

Staying sharp and fresh requires being thankful for all that the King's prophetic voice has been saying and doing in you, and yet believing there's still more! There's more you have not yet experienced.

Second Kings 6:1-7 shares a curious story with some profound wisdom for staying on the cutting edge. Basically, there's a school of the prophetic under the leadership of Elisha, which I'd say we are all part of—the Holy Spirit School of the Supernatural, which I referred to earlier. I don't think we ever graduate from growing as we pursue God's voice. It's an ongoing adventure from glory to glory.

So in short, the prophetic school was doing well and expanding, and the students themselves were growing. As they grew, they needed "more space for themselves." The prophets asked if they could build a new and bigger space for themselves, to which Elisha agreed. They asked Elisha to go with them to build, and he went. They began cutting down trees and doing the work of building the ministry. As they built though, one of the students lost the iron axe-head off his axe. He was particularly worried about this, as it wasn't his axe. In those days, an iron axe was an expensive essential tool, and they couldn't just pop down to Walmart or Costco and grab a new one.

Did You Lose Your Cutting Edge?

Here's where the story takes a supernatural turn that applies to all of us. Elisha asked the prophet where he lost the axe-head. In other words, where did you lose your cutting edge? When he showed him the place in the river, Elisha grabbed a stick and threw it in the water in the same place where the axe-head was lost in the waters. Miraculously, the heavy iron axe-head floated to the top of the water. Then Elisha told the prophet *"'Pick it up for yourself.' So he reached out his hand and took it"* (2 Kings 6:7 NKJV).

The lesson for the prophet? It was important to go back to where he lost the axe-head (his cutting edge) and pick it up for himself.

Nobody else can give us or loan us their anointing or cutting edge. We have to extend our own faith and reach out ourselves for more—it's a personal decision to believe again. And if we find ourselves in a season when we feel like we've lost something and are dull, we have to stretch out our faith to get it back. When we realize we're swinging a blunt tool or a stick without an axe-head, we must ask ourselves where we lost our passion and edge:

- Did I camp around comfortable and fear rather than choosing the fire?

- Did I stop being hungry for more?

- Have I let the distractions of life or the very real challenges of the season to stunt my faith? Have disappointments left me blunt?

- Did the Lord ask something of me and I still have not obeyed or stepped out yet?

- Did I get complacent with the fire on the altar of my heart and neglect to pour fresh fuel on my heart?

- Have I simply forgotten God still restores what is lost?

Whether the enemy stole it or life got in the way, God is well able to restore our cutting edge—and it's His joy to do so. When we feel dry, weary, stale, blunt, or if we feel as if something is missing, there's hope. Sometimes losing our axe-head looks like a holy frustration and desperation within for more. Sometimes it's the feeling of missing God's manifested presence in our life. Sometimes, it's knowing He's calling us back to restore our soul and revive us again.

The Lord is inviting us to receive new sharpness in Him. I hear the King saying, "I'm restoring what was lost. I'm restoring your edge to cut through. Stretch out your hand and pick up new faith. Stretch out your faith and ask Me to lead you into more. Stretch out your hope again and believe for new breakthroughs. I have not forgotten you, My faithful friend."

The invitation is to believe again, press in again, and enter new cutting-edge effectiveness that moves you from mundane and ordinary, to extraordinary.

Mentoring Moment with the King

Take a quiet moment and ask yourself:

- Is there anything holding me back from the invitation in this season of renewed resolution for the fire, even if it costs, and seeking cutting-edge effectiveness?

- Is God highlighting anything to discard or anything to pick back up again? What does that look like for you? Take time to be vulnerable with the Lord and answer the invitation to more. Remind yourself that God is taking you into the extraordinary; and dream with Him about what that looks like for you.

- What doors of opportunity is God inviting you to walk through that will add life to your heart, family, and call?
- Where has fear held you back?
- And where is God inviting fresh cutting-edge courage? Let hope arise as you dream again.

Activation Prayer

Lord, I thank You for inviting me into a new freshness in You. I drop the places that are blunt and dry, and I pick up sharp clarity and restored vision. Lord, would You pour fresh oil on my heart, restore the joy of my salvation, and help me to dream again with You? I partner with all that You are stirring in me and allow Your Spirit to breathe life to the dry bones in my life. Arise, my soul! I don't want to go where Your presence doesn't lead—but where Your presence leads, I choose to boldly go. I receive you as the Lion and the Lamb in my life. I say yes and amen to the invitations Your prophetic voice is leading me into. Revive me again, Lord! Stir the fire like never before. Thank You for Your presence and peace resting upon me and Your smile upon my life. I love You, Jesus. Amen.

15

THE HARVEST AND THE SUPERNATURAL

I T'S HARVEST SEASON, AND EVERYTHING GOD HAS BEEN saying to you is for this moment in time. He's brilliantly prepared you for the harvest of promise and harvest of souls. The supernatural accelerates harvest in your life.

In Acts 2 after the Holy Spirit was poured out, the first thing the Holy Spirit did was talk to everyone about Jesus. Did you get that? The first thing the Holy Spirit did was evangelize. Peter, under the unction of the Holy Spirit, preached in the open and more than 3,000 people believed in Jesus that day.

As we discussed previously, the Holy Spirit drew a crowd with unusual sounds of rushing wind, and people all over the city heard the gospel spoken in their language in miraculous ways. Fire appeared and supernatural joy broke out, causing many to even think the followers of Jesus were drunk, others mocked them, but many more had a personal encounter with the living God.

The city was alive. God certainly drew a crowd and people were talking about the miracles, signs and wonders—and people were paying attention. The observable fire of Pentecost was being poured out, and souls were being saved. This is normal Christianity!

The Supernatural Partnered with Winning the Harvest

Throughout the early church, seeing angels was normal. So normal, in fact, that when Peter was released from jail and approached the home where the disciples were praying, they were more inclined to think an angel was knocking than Peter. And from this place of expecting the supernatural to go hand in hand with preaching the gospel, they went into all the world and shared the Good News of Jesus.

Jesus sent His disciples with the power and fire of God into the harvest fields to reach real people with real hope and real supernatural signs and wonders following the telling of the Gospel. The supernatural was always intended to partner with winning the harvest.

THE HARVEST IS NOT JUST RIPE, IT'S DESPERATE.

Nothing has changed from those times to these times, except we find ourselves in a season I describe as desperate. For sure, this season is intense and the hour urgent. The King's prophetic voice has been, and is speaking to His people through all means to get us ready—for such a time as this. If you know

Jesus, then you know the urgency to be right with God and then run our race with passion and resolve right now.

The harvest is not just ripe, it's desperate. Never in my life-time have I witnessed people so open and desperate to hear the gospel. God has certainly made hearts ready, and people are aware of their own mortality like never before—and they are urgently seeking eternal security. Probably the only thing we can thank the fear-mongering mainstream media for is awakening people to their own mortality. People are fearful and hopeless—and Jesus is the only answer.

THERE IS A WINDOW OF OPPORTUNITY TO STRIKE THE GROUND FOR REVIVAL HARVEST.

My husband and I have seen more salvations in this last short season than we have seen in any other season of our ministry, including when we hosted and led the Pineapple Revival. Certainly the message of the hour is we must have a move of God in our nations, and we must preach the simpleness of the gospel.

Revival, as in nation-shaking revival, is brewing, and the devil is scared. Wherever hungry, praying people are found at the moment, revival is breaking out. There is a window of opportunity to strike the ground and see unprecedented awakening and the long-prophesied harvest of billions of souls.

Truly God has been, and is, getting us ready. The King's prophetic voice has been stretching, growing, healing, and extending the tent pegs of your faith for this very moment. We not only need to recognize what He is saying to us, but we need to apply it and fearlessly run our race. The supernatural voice of God has stirred in you what you need to win a harvest in your sphere of influence.

RIGHT NOW THERE IS GREAT FAVOR OVER EFFORTS TO WIN SOULS.

Let me be really clear to make this point. Right now God is emphasizing the harvest. Souls coming into the Kingdom are the highest priority always, but right now there is a grace and wind blowing over efforts to reach the lost who need salvation. And just like in Acts 2, the Holy Spirit continues to be brilliant at drawing a crowd through signs, wonders, and miracles. Right now there is great favor over efforts to win souls. And God is backing up those going to the harvest fields with supernatural power. I believe where we will see the most and greatest expressions of His prophetic voice, will be in the harvest fields—the marketplace, families, streets, businesses, and community places where everyday people gather and are not just ripe, but desperate. The supernatural was always intended to partner with winning the harvest—this has not changed!

The expression of the supernatural, the ways God's prophetic voice has spoken to you, the miracles you have seen, the ways you uniquely hear Him—all of this will be used by God to reach those around you in this season of abundant harvest of souls. People are desperate, and God is going to use all of us to bring in the harvest, by simply being ourselves.

But I say this, God is chasing down the lost and tired and broken. Many times, if not all the time, they will have experienced something "supernatural or strange or prophetic" already. The harvest already has an expectation of God as supernatural because His prophetic voice has been speaking to them and wooing them. Let's give them the God they are looking for—loving, powerful, supernatural—Savior of all who call on His Name.

The Lion and the Bear

We are being made ready just like David the shepherd was being prepared to become king one day. The lion and bear prepared David for Goliath. I often wonder, *What if David had seen the bear as he watched the sheep and ignored it as an inconsequential distraction, or when he saw the lion he disregarded it as an unnecessary use of his time to be bothered fighting the lion?* Of course he didn't hesitate to act and save the sheep, and in doing so, David was preparing himself for the Goliath that was to come. As we face our lions and bears, we are being readied too.

The King's prophetic voice has been intentionally and lovingly preparing us for the Goliaths of the seasons to come, and the season that is here. Every supernatural sign, every encounter, every dream, vision or manifestation of the glory realm, every prophetic nudge from His voice, every unusual prophetic symbolism that led you on a journey of searching out a matter, even every screenshot of numbers that spoke to you, all of it has been the lion and the bear. It was growing your faith for the supernatural, which you need to run your race.

The supernatural is a faith accelerator for modern-day mountains that must be moved out of the way. Every trial you've walked through was equipping you for what you are stepping into now. We need to hear, recognize, and apply the voice of the King on the run these days. We need to know that the God who spoke to us through an angelic visitation or vivid dream is the same God who will get us through this season of what looks impossible.

THE SUPERNATURAL IS A FAITH ACCELERATOR.

The God who keeps chasing us down with numbers like 2222 and 333 and 1111, is the same God who will go with you while you pray over a hospital full of sick people needing miracles or your sick family member who needs healing. The God who grew your faith by opening your eyes to see visions or your ears to hear trumpets, alarms or heavenly sounds, is the same God who will put words in your mouth as you face those who mock or persecute you. The feathers, oil, encounters you can't fully explain, and the Voice in the fire are all faith accelerators for modern-day mountains that must fall to the ground. The King's prophetic voice has been getting you ready.

Goliath-Slaying Season Is Open

Battling the lion and bear has readied you. Goliath-slaying season is open. The harvest is not just ripe, but truly desperate. And all God has put in us up until now is for them—a harvest that is desperate. To know Him is to love Him, and to love Him is to serve Him. He has been speaking to your heart from before you were born calling you by name for such a time as now.

How you hear Him, see Him, feel Him, connect with Him—people all around us need to know the same God that you have come to know through His prophetic voice. Your story of how you hear God is an anointed weapon in the harvest.

Seeing Numbers Leading People to God

As I shared earlier, just seeing numbers repetitively, like 1111, 316, or 2222, is leading people to find Jesus, many through our targeted ministry online. While some debate if God can speak in unusual ways like numbers, people are finding Jesus through His creative voice. It constantly amazes me how God chases after hearts. Those who see the opportunity of the season are reaping a harvest.

The Family of God Is Quickly Expanding

God's family is expanding and quickly. Those who are joining us are not interested in our squabbles with each other; they just need a family who talks like the Father they've already been hearing. God has been speaking to the harvest through the Man in white in their dreams, or the number sequence they keep seeing, or the angel they saw in their sleep, or the supernatural encounter they couldn't explain, or the ache in their heart for real love. They've felt a desperation for eternal security and peace and a need to find the God who's been calling them home for a lifetime. They are looking for the God who talks because He's already been speaking to them in many different ways already.

> THE DEVIL HAS TRICKED GOD'S PEOPLE INTO FOCUSING ON THE NATURAL, WHILE THE HARVEST IS LOOKING FOR THE SUPERNATURAL.

We're about to hear and see miracles we've never heard of before. We are about to see God move in ways we don't have words for. We're about to see souls, souls, souls come into the Kingdom in traditional and nontraditional ways in numbers that will blow our minds. We have been prepared for this hour, to properly introduce them to the God whose voice they have already been hearing, wooing them to Himself. Don't be surprised when you hear more and more wild stories of God's prophetic voice getting the attention of the unsaved.

Church Came to Her

The following several stories are shared for encouragement and inspiration. This first one is heavy, but real and hopeful.

We were eating lunch at a Mexican restaurant after church and someone I knew came running up to our table and asked us to come outside and pray with a friend. Her friend had very sadly seen her sister die in traumatic circumstances and had been told not to attend church by her family—but her friend knew God was the answer she desperately needed. When we reached the car, it was obvious the young woman was profoundly distraught. Fear and grief was tangible. Thank God for friends who don't give up.

We asked her if we could pray, and then spoke peace and prayed God's heart over her. She had been shaking for days, and although she was touched by the prayer, nothing much was changed physically that we could see. Yet I heard God say, "She needs Me." This is when hearing the prophetic voice of the King really matters.

We then explained that the hope she needed was a Person and asked if she would like to invite Jesus into her life, then we simply explained the gospel. She replied that she was not religious and didn't want to do that. I responded, "Well that's good, because I'm not religious either. I love God because He's real, and a relationship with Him changed my life; I hear and feel Him. Would you like us to pray for the real God, a living God, to come inside you and help?"

"Yes," her answer came straightaway. We prayed and she prayed with us. As soon as we prayed for the Holy Spirit to come and fill her, her head jolted backward suddenly, she yelled, breathed deeply, and then looked at us, shocked at what happened. She literally felt God come into her life!

She knew God's presence suddenly. Her eyes teared up. I was crying. We all were crying. There was still a journey, but I knew she had God's love and presence inside now, and so did she. I was deeply moved that a girl so fearful, scared, and traumatized, unable to attend church and scared of what could happen when people who believed in God prayed, was courageous enough, desperate enough, to search out God anyway. The harvest is not just ripe, it's desperate. And I was glad that day for the bears and lions that had helped get us ready. I was glad in that moment for the bear and the lion that trained me to hear God in the heat of the moment.

Killing Myself Tattoo

I'd just finished preaching and praying for many, and the building was now nearly empty. A staff member asked if I could pray for a lady sitting at the back of church. She was a known drug addict and clearly was not doing well. As I walked up to her, I could feel an invisible force field pushing me away, but this encouraged me to press in all the more. I asked if I could pray for her and, despite not looking me in the eye, she said yes.

She did not want to be in church and kept saying she hated God and hated church. When I asked why was she here, she repeatedly said, "I don't want to live, I don't want to live." My heart was gripped with the urgency of the situation before me. I knew there was a war going on inside her, a war that we needed to win right now. I immediately knew in my spirit that this was the last chance she had. I can't explain how deeply I felt the urgency for her salvation, and I knew I was going to battle for this one.

Across her chest was a tattoo of many words, but ones that stuck in my head were, "killing myself is the only end." This woman—who was visibly broken, diseased, demonized, and said she hated God—had walked into the church that day because God drew her, despite her pain. He had been speaking to her since before she was born, and calling her by name. That day, as I looked at her with tears streaming down my face, I prophesied, I prayed, I listened to the Lord intently and spoke what I heard. I listened for the prophetic voice of the King. I knew she needed Jesus. I knew she needed Him now. I could feel death knocking, and I knew I was standing in the way.

The Lord spoke to me about how she had been hurt and abandoned by her mother, and I told her God wanted her to know that was not His heart for her. The words she had heard were not how He thought about her. I saw a vision of her crying as I hugged her, so I asked if I could give her a hug, like a mother would; and though she drew backward, she said yes. I held her tight and whispered in her ear, "God loves you and He has a plan for you."

As I hugged her she began to cry. She also miraculously began to sober up. I looked her straight in the eye and told her that God brought her here today because He loves her, wants to live inside her, and make a home in her. That she wasn't alone. I explained very simply who Jesus is and asked if she would like to say yes to Jesus living inside her. She said again, "I hate God."

I knew if I walked away, this was her last chance. The reality of the battle was urgent. I couldn't stop fighting for her. I couldn't let go. I was compelled to seek God for keys to her heart—He gave me words and pictures that spoke healing to broken, abused places.

I boldly looked her in the eye again and said, "Those demons are lying to you. They want to keep you from meeting the One who loves you and has hope for you. They want to keep you trapped in torment. Do you want the torment to stop?"

"Yes," she whispered.

"Do you want Jesus to make a home in you?"

"Yes," she said. We prayed together, and she even prayed to forgive her mum, as she gave Jesus her life.

As I hugged her, she breathed deeply, she sighed in a way I knew peace had come. Then—incredibly, she hugged me, and tightly. I knew there was still a long journey, but I knew the One who called her since before she was born, now made His home in her.

The harvest is not just ripe, it's desperate. I'll see her in Heaven one day. And I can tell you this, I was glad that day for the bear and the lion, for they helped get me ready for the heat of the battle.

Online Media Ministry

Consistently, we are seeing the same things happen online. People being healed, delivered, and saying yes to Jesus with increasing desperation and numbers. I'm mentioning this because media is a mission field that God is using in more and more radical ways to win the lost and minister to the lonely and scared. Just in the last year, at the time of writing this, my husband and I have seen multiple thousands receive Jesus through online ministry, including through GOD TV.

Examples of just a few of the many miracles as a result of the King's prophetic voice through media: a woman healed of early onset dementia, people fighting Covid experienced immediate release of chest pressure, visible tumors shrank, physical pain ceased, fear broke, people jumped out of bed feeling well who had been bedridden in pain, backs were healed, migraines broken, and the list goes on.

This kind of ministry is interactive so we can get immediate feedback from those receiving prayer via comments. Often as we minster online we will feel heat or pain in our bodies, which is always a sign to us that God is healing someone in this part of their body; and as we release what God has revealed, we receive comments from the people confirming, "Yes, God just healed me!"

And all this is recorded in the Bible. Matthew 8:8-10 (TPT) tells us:

> *But the Roman officer interjected, "Lord, who am I to have you come into my house? I understand your authority, for I too am a man who walks under authority and have authority over soldiers who serve under me. I can tell one to go and he'll go, and another to come and he'll come. I command my servants and they'll do whatever I ask. So I know that all you need to do is to stand here and command healing over my son and he will be instantly healed." Jesus was astonished when he heard this and said to those who were following him, "He has greater faith than anyone I've encountered in Israel!"*

I love these verses as it shows how online/media ministry works in the Kingdom: "*...all you need to do is stand here and command healing...and he will be instantly healed.*" The Kingdom works by authority. Another reason I love this passage is because it also speaks about how Jesus was astonished at the officer's faith!

Astonishing Jesus with Our Faith

May we be a generation that astonishes Jesus with our faith! May we be the generation that stands with our hands on hospital walls and sees the entire hospital cleared out of sick and dying people. May we be the generation that sees the glory cloud sweep in overnight to our cities and our neighbors found in the front yard crying out, "What must I do to be saved?" May we be the generation that sees a nation saved in a day and resurrection power restored as normal. May we astonish Jesus with our faith, just as Jesus was astonished at the Roman soldier's faith who said that Jesus could command healing from afar and knew it would be so. We need this kind of faith. The harvest needs us to have this kind of faith.

A Grandmother Tormented by Fear

I remember speaking to a grandmother on the phone who, for years, had been tormented by noises and dark, fearful, demonic encounters in her home. She had tried everything she knew to do to rid her home of the torment that, sadly, involved endless and useless New Age, powerless rituals. The crystals, the cards, the superstitious sayings, none of it helped. She was scared and fearful of not only this life, but the life to come, as she had no peace and didn't know how to find it.

As I explained the simpleness of the gospel, Jesus started breaking lies and fears from her life and revealing pictures to me of past events that God wanted to heal. As we prayed together, she found Jesus and the fear and torment was evicted in Jesus' name.

The woman found peace in Jesus and was no longer afraid to die—or live. The demonic tried to entrap, but Jesus led this grandmother to freedom in Him. The demons were lying to her, but I heard the King's prophetic voice speak clearly how to cut her free. I'll see her in Heaven one day. And again, I sure am glad for the lion and the bear that prepared me for that day.

Her Back Was Healed

Not long ago, I stood in the mud in an open field during a revival tent crusade with a lady who was hurting. Her younger sister told me that she had been in extreme pain from an injury for 16 years. I felt pressure in my back, which I knew was not mine, so it encouraged me to keep praying till I felt that go, even though we had been praying a long time already. And then the pain began to shift and I felt a release in my body, so we prayed again.

I knew she was healed when I saw her smile for the first time. I asked how she felt and she could only cry, "It's gone, it's gone!" I looked at the sister and she was weeping, saying, "You don't understand—she can't even get out of bed most days, so to come here was hard. I don't remember a time when she was not in pain." I cried then too.

Jesus, my Healer! He is so worthy. I looked at the woman and knew it was done. And I thought to myself, *I'm so glad for the bear and the lion that readied me for the muddy fields of battle so I can stand with the desperate and give them Jesus.*

The times God has grown us through hearing His prophetic voice, the signs, the symbols, the dreams, the unusual—all of it—it's been making us ready.

The Harvest Is Ripe and Desperate

The King's prophetic voice has been preparing us for the greatest move of God that has ever been. The season has been dark and challenges remain, but the Lord has been busy reminding all of us that He is greater.

You, my friend, are part of the end-time army—the glorious, victorious church that will see a harvest of souls happen in unprecedented numbers. This includes your family and loved ones you've been praying for faithfully. Despite the devil's best efforts, the glory of the Lord will cover the earth. Revival is breaking out all around the world right now, and increasingly God is using all of us to be ourselves and run our race, reaching desperate people with God's love and salvation.

The bears and the lions you've conquered—whether trials by fire, intense challenge, or hearing God's prophetic voice in ways that stretched you—has prepared you for what we're stepping into. The harvest needs what you carry and who you are. Those searching for God will need the benefit of your battled-tested experience with the bear and the lion. Those who are coming will need your wisdom about how the King speaks in creative ways. The harvest is coming, and you can show them our supernatural God who still defeats modern-day Goliaths. Let me be clear—we are going to hear some wild stories of God moving and see some out-of-the-box miracles and expressions of the King's prophetic voice we haven't even dreamed of yet. To build your faith, God's been showing you He's bigger and wilder than you thought—so you can embrace a people about to come in who are looking for the supernatural God Almighty, the King of kings.

Take It In and Pour It Out

God's prophetic voice is speaking to you, friend. He's been calling you, loving you, and speaking to you since before you were born. These are the days you were born for, and you will hear His voice say which way to go. You've got this! Whatever and however God has shown you that He's alive, supernatural, and powerful, take it all in and then pour it out on others. The harvest is looking for the real God—the God who has prepared you so you can show them that bears and lions still bow to the name of Jesus. Goliaths still fall. The harvest is looking for what you have—the real Jesus.

Mentoring Moment with the King

- Who in your sphere of influence has God placed on your heart who needs Jesus?

- How can you pray for them?

- What bears and lions has God used to get you ready for this season?

- In thinking about the kind of faith that astonishes Jesus, what kind of testimonies and miracle stories stir you to believe for more?

- What can you contend for that you haven't seen yet?

- What is a harvest goal you can set for this season?

- How can you pray for your family and nation?

Your Commissioning Prayer for the Harvest

My fiery friend, I bless you as you pour it out. As you take the lessons you learned from conquering the bears and lions, from hearing the prophetic voice of the King, from the supernatural ways God has readied you, I charge you to pour out God's power and love on those around you. I bless you with fire. I bless you with Holy Spirit power. I bless you with signs, wonders, and miracles following. I bless you with His presence leading you and moving in and through you. I bless you with favor, grace, and breakthrough. I bless you with encounters with King Jesus that transform you and compel you to seek His face. You are called, anointed, and appointed for now, and I mark you with radical, fiery, contagious encounters. I charge you to run to the harvest in your sphere of influence and give them Jesus. You're ready. Go pour out what God has given you—Jesus' love and power. The prophetic voice of the King has prepared you and empowered you. I call in a mighty harvest of souls and miracles that will astound you, beginning in your own family. Be blessed as you pour it out. Amen.

16

818 COMMISSION

Isaiah 8:18 TPT

Behold—here I stand, and the children whom the Lord Yahweh has given me are for signs and wonders in Israel, sent from the Lord Almighty, Commander of Angel Armies, who is enthroned on Mount Zion!

You are a sign and a wonder sent from the Lord Almighty, Commander of Angel Armies, to this generation.

Deuteronomy 8:18 NKJV

And you shall remember the Lord your God, for it is He who gives you power to get wealth, that He may establish His covenant which He swore to your fathers, as it is this day.

God is giving you the power to create wealth and establish promise.

ROMANS 8:18 TPT

I am convinced that any suffering we endure is less than nothing compared to the magnitude of glory that is about to be unveiled within us.

The glory is increasing upon you.
You have a glorious destiny
that outweighs the suffering.
You, my friend, are a sign and wonder of
His glory on display to this generation.

During the past season, and especially while writing this book, I very often saw the number 818! Examples include being upgraded in our hotel to room 818 or sent a significant word at 8:18 p.m. As I got up to make my coffee today at around 6 a.m., the clock on our coffee machine was randomly flashing 8:18! It must have been unplugged and the clock needed to be reset, but it was such a cool prophetic sign as I write this.

For months, my husband and I have been seeing the number 818 quite frequently. Like many times when God speaks to us, it becomes a bit of a laugh, as suddenly a particular number seems to chase us down. Like many times before, I've simply asked the Holy Spirit to reveal what He is saying to me.

NO SEASON IS WITHOUT HOPE OR HIS VOICE.

I knew God was highlighting Deuteronomy 8:18 and talking about the power to get or create wealth, but I knew this meant more than just finances. Both Ben and I were feeling stirred to believe for increased capacity to create finances for the Kingdom endeavors God was speaking to us about, so Deuteronomy 8:18 became a specific declaration in our lives. Shortly afterward, an opportunity arose for a short-term business project that has blessed us financially. We believe that came from specifically decreeing 818 blessing over our call and finances.

I knew there was more, however. The King's prophetic voice has been preparing a generation for the season we are stepping into. Every time we hear His voice, our faith has been strengthened and/or the supernatural realm has stretched us and imparted new levels of authority—getting us ready.

THE KING HAS MADE YOU A LITERAL SIGN AND WONDER TO THIS GENERATION.

The signs and the wonders have not just spoken a message to you—they have *made you* the message! You have become a literal sign and wonder of God's glory to this generation. Your sphere of influence needs the anointing and the authority that the King's prophetic voice has been diligently imparting to you. He has made you ready. He has made you a sign and a wonder on earth for this generation.

People around you need hope like never before. Specifically, they need what God has been pouring into you. All the supernatural encounters, the prophetic symbolism and glory realm interactions have birthed a faith in you that God is bigger than the natural circumstances. Your story speaks hope to others. Your encounters release faith to those around you. The way God has moved in you, He wants to move in others. You are a signpost that points to Jesus.

Many years ago, I remember a minster prophesied over me, "You, Jodie, don't just see signs and wonders, you ARE a sign and wonder." At the time it didn't make sense to me at all. I had seen many signs and wonders, but God was still growing faith. Within weeks, though, my husband and I were awakened in the night by an angel standing on the end of our bed; and as you know, everything changed. This visitation heralded in an entirely new season for us. Pour It Out Ministries was birthed, and we ministered worldwide, releasing revival and seeing people come to God.

What God does in you becomes contagious as it breaks out in others. God was using us to release His presence and power in the nations, with signs, wonders, and miracles following. We were beginning to grasp that what God had done in us—the encounters He was pouring out in our lives—were contagious, and were increasingly breaking out in our meetings and through our personal lives.

> GOD ISN'T WAITING ON A SEASON—
> HE'S WAITING ON A PEOPLE.

I knew that God was calling a people to not just experience the power of God and hear His voice, but to carry the same message to a generation desperate for God's miraculous power to break in. God isn't waiting on a season, He's waiting on a people. A people is arising in this season who *are* signs and wonders on the earth, pointing people to Jesus and pointing people to the God of all things are possible. A great harvest is imminent.

As I continued to see 818, I knew there was more God was talking to me about. God also began highlighting Romans 8:18 and talking to me about His increasing glory about to be poured out.

> *I am convinced that any suffering we endure is less than nothing compared to the magnitude of glory that is about to be unveiled within us* (Romans 8:18 TPT).

The 818 Commission for a People

I am now stirred every time I see 818, as it has become a prophetic word for the hour. God is marking a people with the 818 Commission.

In summary, this is what I see God releasing to a people by highlighting 818. These verses: Deuteronomy 8:18, Romans 8:18, and Isaiah 8:18 have different emphases, but I believe they all share a similar message that speaks hope to what seems to have no hope. Signs and wonders point to Jesus, and God is making a people as signs and wonders on earth to testify of His glory. The glory outweighs the suffering of this present season, and it will again mark a people in an observable way as His weighty glory increases.

God is giving power to create and establish wealth, even in new, unusual ways, to walk in the fullness of promise. A wave of new ideas, projects, Kingdom reforming ministries, supernatural exploits, unseen before miracles, entrepreneurial enterprises, and culture shifting endeavors will arise. This, all of this, makes this people a walking sign and wonder to a generation in need of hope.

818 Commission for You

You are a sign and a wonder of His glory to this generation. I believe God is marking a people to walk in this commission in these days. Decree this as you read:

> My friend, God is marking you as a sign and a wonder sent from the Lord Almighty, Commander of Angel Armies, to this generation. What you carry is transferable, and you have become a message of hope and miraculous power to those around you. You have seen God's signs and wonders, but God is making you a sign and a wonder in the hour that points to Jesus and gives a generation hope that God is still the God of all things are possible. He will use you to create and restore wealth, restoring what the enemy has stolen. God will stretch your capacity to carry divine ideas and wealth solutions that will enable you to walk in the promises of God over your life.
>
> As doors close, God is imparting anointing to a people to establish new doors of opportunity and provision. The glory realm is increasing, and His glory will cover the earth. God is imparting to you faith for a glorious future, and His glory will

outweigh the suffering of the season. Look for His glory. Contend for His glory, as the hope of the season is carried by a people who know their God is powerful, regardless of the circumstances. The fall-face-down glory (see Ezekiel 44:4) will not just mark you, but mark a generation. God is calling you, and imparting to you, a commission to carry His glory in this hour. You have seen many signs and wonders; now God is commissioning you to be a sign and a wonder in this generation who imparts hope that all things are still possible with God. His glory is increasing.

Be encouraged, friend. I believe God is imparting fresh anointing on His people to walk in an 818 anointing for this season. But it's more than this. Everything the King's prophetic voice has released and established in you, you will carry to others. Say with me, "I have seen signs, wonders, and miracles. I have heard my King's prophetic voice—and God is establishing me as a sign and wonder in my generation of His glory. I point to Jesus, the God of signs, wonders, and miracles still."

Mentoring Moment with the King

As you read over these 818 verses, decree them to your circumstances. Allow the Holy Spirit to highlight what resonates with you to contend for and release in this season to your family, city, and region. Ask yourself what this looks like in your family and in those in your sphere of influence. What new faith is God stirring in you to contend for in this season?

Activation Prayer

King Jesus, we need You now more than ever. Thank You for Your glory. Thank You for Your voice. Thank You for Your supernatural power and presence in our lives. Use me as a sign and wonder in my family and community to point people to hope in You. Use me as a catalyst of faith. I speak forth signs, wonders, and miracles to break out in my life and circumstances. Thank You for anointing me and commissioning me to be a sign and wonder of Your glory realm, releasing hope to others that You are the God of all things are possible. May my life point people to Jesus and lead people to Your love in increasing measure. Amen.

17

FROM PROPHETIC MESSAGE TO ACTIVATION

R EVELATION FINDS ITS PURPOSE WHEN ACTED ON. THIS chapter includes a practical guide with tips for how to actually activate the prophetic messages you've received into your everyday life. Blessings, prayers, and practical keys are also shared in this concluding chapter designed to enhance your journey with the King's prophetic voice today, and for years to come.

Childlike Hunger and Faith

I am big on childlike hunger and faith. Every encounter, supernatural sign, or symbolic way the King's prophetic voice has spoken to you are all personal messages from the King.

Every time God has intercepted my world with His prophetic voice, and anytime I have wondered what He was saying to me in a supernatural way, ultimately the meaning has come from simply asking God, "What are You saying to me?" and waiting for God to show me.

It's this simplicity of seeking God for answers and revelation that I have most wanted to impart to you throughout this book. I pray that you've found that childlike joy of discovery all over again. My prayer is that your relationship with God is never boring and always full of wonder. God is the Mystery Revealer, and He will continue to reveal the hidden things to you as you seek Him.

> THE KEY THAT SETS APART THOSE WHO WALK IN THEIR CALL IS THAT THEY EMBRACE AND ACTIVATE THE PROPHETIC MESSAGE.

Prophetic friend, when God speaks to you, He is delivering a personal message to you. The key that sets apart those who actually enter into their prophetic Promised Land, is that they embrace the prophetic message God is communicating, and then actually activate it. Put simply—do something with it! As we activate what God says and implement change in practical ways into our journey with Him, we advance into purpose and promise.

If we don't embrace the revelatory message and activate what God is saying, we lose the potency of the wisdom given. Through activation, faith arises and breakthrough comes. To enter our destiny, we must *do something* with God's prophetic voice, not just hear it.

Activation puts boots on the King's prophetic voice to take new ground. The message may have come in a mystical, supernatural way, but often the walking out of what He's saying is far more pragmatic.

God loves you, friend, and desires the glory realm to impact your circumstances, relationships, and everything you put your hand to.

God has entrusted you with His prophetic voice. He equally empowers you to step into and activate His prophetic voice in your life.

The following simple questions and prompts will help you work out practical ways you can activate what God has been saying to you.

Activation Keys

1. *Activate the Message of the Prophetic Encounter*

When you know God is speaking a message to you, it's time to intentionally believe God to walk in the fruit of what He's speaking to you. When God is repeatedly showing you the same message, consider it to be an important and necessary key for your next season that should be embraced fully.

Take a moment and ask yourself the following questions. Not every question will apply, but be real and candid. Journaling your responses will help reveal themes and consistent wisdom provided by God for your season:

- What and how is God most often speaking to me?
- What is the main thing the encounters and prophetic words received are saying to me?
- What practical process can I implement in my life to walk out what God is saying in a fresh or more fruitful way?

- Are there changes or course corrections I need to make?
- Is God highlighting any Bible verses or stories to me I can meditate on specifically?
- Is God giving me a prayer focus or directive?
- Who or what is on God's heart in this encounter? Can I partner with Him in a practical way to release God's heart over what God is talking to me about?
- What is the main theme God is stirring in me to grow?
- Can I shift my focus in practical ways to embrace the wisdom God is giving, and what does that look like in my life?
- Are there decrees and prayers I can focus on for this season?
- Is there strategy, discernment, or insight God is giving me?
- What perspective shifts in my thinking do I need to embrace to walk this out?
- What wisdom has God added to my current situation?
- Has God imparted new or fresh anointing to me? What for? How can I take a practical step to activate that anointing in my life?
- Can I do something creative that will partner with stirring up the things God is saying?

- Can I do a practical, prophetic act that will partner in faith with what God saying?

- Who can I share with what God is saying to me and give testimony to how God is stretching me?

- Is there anything God is highlighting for me to grow in or study in the Scriptures? What is a simple way I can start doing that?

- What is God speaking to my heart? How can I steward my heart well in this season?

- Are there any lies, limitations, or fears God is highlighting for me to evict? What is God saying I have done well and encouraging me in?

- As God talks to me about new capacity, new anointing, or new pioneering projects, what is one actionable plan I can make to move forward in the new?

- What one practical step can I implement into my daily life/season that will honor what God is speaking to me?

- In a nutshell, what is the main thing God is talking to me about through His prophetic voice?

Remember, there are no right or wrong answers. This is simply intended to help you think and process what and how God has spoken to you and to steward His voice well.

2. Long-Term Goals Are Not the Same as Actionable Steps

Taking the process of activation even further, narrow down all God is saying to you and write down one practical step to move forward in the direction of what God is saying.

It's important that your practical step be actionable, or you won't do it. Long-term goals are necessary and powerful, but to move forward short term, doable steps are needed. Taking a practical step forward breaks inertia or fear and activates God's word in our lives. Take the long-term goal or dream that the King's prophetic voice has birthed in you and break it down into actionable, simple steps that you can and will implement. This begins the process of activating the prophetic message into your life.

Remember, to enter our destiny we have to *do something* with what God is saying to us. This only needs to be a small step of faith, as God honors our small beginnings.

- What is the big picture God is talking to you about?
- What is one simple, actionable, practical step you can take right now?

3. Turn Your Prophetic Message Into a Prayer of Activation

In First Timothy 1:18 (NLT) Paul says, "…*here are my instructions for you, based on the prophetic words spoken about you earlier. May they help you fight well in the Lord's battles.*"

What this is talking about is taking our prophetic words and messages from God and using them to *"fight the good fight"* (1 Timothy 6:12 NIV) by reminding ourselves what God is speaking to us. In other words, turn the King's prophetic message to you into a prayer that activates faith for the days to come. Invite God to activate you into bold courage and cutting-edge wisdom to overcome and conquer. Take what He is saying to you and pray it out as a war cry that scatters the enemy and a declaration of breakthrough.

Every time His supernatural realm intersects with your natural world, God is not just speaking a cool message, but imparting power to activate it and actually live it. Remember, when God speaks to us in any way, He's building relationship so we trust what He's saying. Allow this to be the start of an ongoing conversation that leads you closer to Jesus, and into *living* the dream, not just dreaming it.

And mostly, know that you are seen and loved by God. The King's prophetic voice calls you, anoints you, and empowers you to live the days of purpose for which you were born. On the other side of revelation are God adventures and victories you haven't even begun to imagine yet. What you've heard and seen is just a taste of what is yet to come as you step into and embrace the King's prophetic voice to you.

Prayer of Blessing and Activation

Please personalize and pray this prayer:

> *Thank You, God, that You are speaking to me. Thank You for what You have been saying to me through* ___

> _____

> *(insert ways God has talked to you and the revelation He has given you here). I welcome Your supernatural glory realm in my life. I welcome Your prophetic voice and wisdom into my heart and life. Thank You for*

empowering me to walk in the practical processes of entering the promise You are stirring in me. Thank You that I will live in closer connection to You in my daily life, knowing Your nearness and tangible presence.

Help me, Lord, to not just hear You, but walk in all You say. I trust You and know Your wisdom will positively affect my call, family, and journey forward. Those in my sphere of influence will be impacted by Your love and Your supernatural interactions with me in life-giving, redemptive ways. Help me to embrace all You are doing in me, and activate the revelation You are pouring into me.

I invite Your Holy Spirit to work in my life, both in my present and future days, aligning my life with the dream and promise of Heaven. I receive all You are saying and stirring in me, and I cherish Your voice in my life. Ignite a fresh fire in me to boldly go where You're leading. I trust You to lead me into the fullness of the days for which I was born.

I love Your voice, God. I love Your prophetic ways. I love You. Amen.

My Blessing to You

My pioneering friend, may you be blessed in your heart, home, and daily life. May you increasingly grow in wisdom and discernment of the King's prophetic voice in your life. I bless you with the fire of His presence, the blazing love of God surrounding you, and the knowledge that God is with you and making a way for you. I bless you with increased capacity to carry and implement all He is speaking to you. I bless you with encounters that speak Heaven's heart to you. I bless you with increased anointing to hear, see, and know the King's voice in your life. I bless you with the ease of childlike joy in your relationship with God.

I bless you with divine health, healing where you need it, and breakthrough in Jesus' name. I bless you with peace and protection all the days of your life. I bless you with the establishing of what God is saying to you in this season and the fullness of promise and breakthrough. May you be blessed in His love today, and the days to come. May you know that you are a sign and a wonder of God's glory to this generation, called by the God of Angel Armies to impact earth with Heaven's miraculous realm.

I bless you with the presence and power of the Kingdom realm. May you be blessed as you embrace the way God whispers and roars over you. May you be blessed with burning-bush encounters that lead to promises fulfilled and blazing passion for divine purpose. You will be one who is known as a friend of the King as you cherish and honor His voice in all His ways. May you forever know that the King's prophetic voice has called you, anointed you, and empowered you for such a time as now. I bless you to increasingly hear, see, and know the King's prophetic voice in profoundly radical ways that mark you, transform you, and impact a generation.

In the precious name of our King Jesus, amen.

Now my friend, take what the King's prophetic voice is saying to you and go live your God dream and blaze a trail others will follow.

Destiny awaits and the King is cheering you on!

PRAYER OF SALVATION

As you read this book, if you have realized God is calling you to say yes to Jesus and surrender your heart and life to Him, I invite you to pray the following prayer today:

Dear Jesus,
I chose right now to give You my life.
Come and live inside me.
I want to be born again!
I believe and thank You that You died on the cross for me and were raised again from the dead.
I repent from all my sins, and ask You to please forgive me.
Thank You for Your forgiveness.
I receive Your forgiveness and love.
Thank You that according to the Bible, I am now a new creation.
The old has gone and the new has come!
Fill me with Your Holy Spirit.
Fill me with Your power and presence.
Thank You that I will hear and know Your voice,
And help me to live every day of my life for You.
Thank You, Jesus!
AMEN!

If you just prayed this prayer and meant it from your heart, I want to be the first to welcome you to the family of God! The Bible says, *"there is rejoicing in the presence of the angels of God over one sinner who repents"* (Luke 15:10 NIV)—so there is a party going on right now in your honor!

Now I encourage you to:

1. Please go to our website and let us know you made this important decision. We would love to hear from you, connect with you and encourage you. Website: www.pouritout.org/yes

2. Tell someone what you have just done.

3. Start to read the Bible, even a little bit every day will be a blessing to you. A great place to start is the book of John in the New Testament.

4. Pray. Prayer is just talking to God. It doesn't require any fancy language or words, just talk to Him as a friend. Ask Him questions, and then listen. Many people find keeping a prayer journal really helpful. Write prayers in the journal, and then stop and listen. God will speak, sometimes in creative ways, as this book has shown you.

5. Read my husband's and my other books. They will help you greatly in your journey forward with God. *The King's Decree* by Jodie Hughes (me) and *When God Breaks In* by Ben Hughes. You can order these from our website at www .pouritout.org

God bless you, friend.

Pour It Out Ministries

NUMBER SEQUENCE MEANING GUIDE

Prophetic Meaning and Insight Into Most Common Number Sequences Receptively Seen

This is a guide to lead you into prophetic understanding of the most common number sequences seen, and their most often meaning. Be aware that prophetic insight is personal, and so use this as a guide, understanding God may reveal additional insight. Equally, meanings may change from season to season, or in different circumstances. This guide gives you revelation, meaning and insight into what God is saying to you through the number sequence seen. Blessings as you discover God's prophetic message to you.

1

1111, 11:11

Awakening; Resurrection Power and Life; Revival; Personal Spiritual Wake-Up Call

> John 11:11 NIV: *"After he had said this, he went on to tell them, 'Our friend Lazarus has fallen asleep; but I am going there to wake him up.'"*

Awakening, wake-up call, fresh spiritual awakening into more, supernatural favor and provision to take possession of promises, transition and alignment, revival. God is bringing life to the dead things and places. God is breathing encounters over you to wake you up into spiritual clarity, fresh connected relationship with Him, and awaken a new sense of identity in God and your exciting eternal purpose. God is waking you up from dull religion to active, alive relationship with Him. God is waking up our nations, families, and those in our sphere of influence to His realness and power to turn around circumstances. God is inviting you to pray with urgency for revival and harvest and to bless what He is already doing. Resurrection power is available in your circumstances.

11 can mean transition and so a doubling of eleven can signify a season of intense shaking as things transition into the new. 11 also means alignment and so the shaking brings alignment to allow for awakening and revival.

Resurrection life, God of the impossible, AWAKENING

Isaiah 11:11 NIV: *"In that day the Lord will reach out his hand a second time to reclaim the surviving remnant of his people...."*

God is with His remnant.

Deuteronomy 11:11 NIV: *"But the land you are crossing the Jordan to take possession of is a land of mountains and valleys that drinks rain from heaven."*

111

Multiplication of Blessing; God Is Faithful to His Promises

Deuteronomy 1:11 NIV: *"May the Lord, the God of your ancestors, increase you a thousand times and bless you as he has promised!"*

Blessing to you and your family. Increase of blessing and inheritance of blessing is yours to call in as you were promised. The blessing you are entering into is greater than you've experienced before. Pray and decree your promises, expecting exponential blessing as an inheritance. Decree a thousand-fold increase over the promises in your life. You are entering a time of sudden and accelerated increase. A call to believe God's faithfulness as He has promised you.

130

The Lord Himself Is Fighting for You

When engaged in warfare for promises that have come under increased attack, be encouraged the Lord is reminding you that He is fighting for you. Trust in His care and power to battle on your behalf. Expect miraculous breakthrough. A call to arise in prayer and believe God is warring alongside you, and on your behalf.

> Deuteronomy 1:30 NIV: *"The Lord your God, who is going before you, will fight for you, as he did for you in Egypt, before your very eyes,"*

153

Evangelism; Souls; Bountiful Harvest; Urgency to Win Souls

> John 21:11 NLT: *"Simon Peter went aboard and dragged the net to the shore. There were 153 large fish, and yet the net hadn't torn."*

Look for the harvest of souls, expect bountiful harvest, urgency of souls, more than you expect. You'll be surprised by how ready people are to receive Jesus as their Savior. God will use you to bring in the harvest and is increasing an evangelism anointing on you. The Lord is expanding your heart for evangelism and people who need salvation. Pray and invite God to give you increased boldness to share the gospel, to use what you have, and expect bountiful results.

2

22, 222, 2222

Open Doors; God Is Opening Doors that Cannot Be Shut;
Increase of Kingdom Authority; Keys Are Being Released to
Unlock Destiny and God Opportunity

> Isaiah 22:22 NIV: *"I [God] will place on his shoulder*
> *the key to the house of David; what he opens no one*
> *can shut, and what he shuts no one can open."*

Open door. Double doors. Authority to decree God's purposes. An assurance of His promises. Keys to the Kingdom. Open doors of favor. Walk through the open door. Humanity cannot stop what God had decreed. Kingly authority to take new ground. Encouragement for the pioneer and those establishing apostolic works to trust and enter new promise. You can trust God with both open and closed doors. Intercede with governmental, kingly authority establishing in the spirit Kingdom order. Pursue in faith what God is releasing. Boldly unlock and overturn unrighteousness, and use your authority to decree and establish God's Word in circumstances around you. A call to take the God destiny doors and advance into destiny.

222

Revealing of Hidden Wisdom and Open Doors of Revelation

> Daniel 2:22 NIV: *"He reveals deep and hidden things;*
> *he knows what lies in darkness, and light dwells with*
> *him."*

Open doors to needed revelation and wisdom. Ask the Lord to reveal wisdom to you as yet that has been hidden. God is shining light that reveals not only deeper understanding and wisdom to you, but exposes darkness and strategies of the enemy. As God exposes the darkness, remember that what God reveals is to heal, and allow His light to create in us a clean heart in even deeper ways. Ask for God's wisdom on a matter. Expect light to reveal and expose the enemy's lies, tactics, and strategies that have hindered your progress and receive new wisdom to advance forward. There is a deeper wisdom God is growing you in. Invite the Lord's wisdom and fear of the Lord to increase in your life and thank Him for anointed wisdom in your circumstances.

211

Listen to the Spirit

> Revelation 2:11 NIV: *"Whoever has ears, let them hear what the Spirit says to the churches...."*

Listen to God. Be spiritually alert and purposefully listen to what God is saying and releasing as God is speaking. Discern God's voice above all other noise. God is growing your discernment. Take note of what God is saying, and be deliberately and specifically aware of His voice. Use discernment and receive His wisdom attentively and obediently.

212

Transformation in the Fire of God

It's hot, but God is with you in the heat! Things are getting hot spiritually and transformation will take place. Let His fire transform your heart and the circumstances around you. 212 degrees Fahrenheit (100 degrees Celsius) is the boiling point for water (at standard atmospheric pressure) implying transformation by heat/fire. Things are heating up and this will bubble over and bring transformation/change. Listen to God's voice attentively as things are transforming around you.

2021

Sent One

John 20:21 NKJV: *"So Jesus said to them again, 'Peace to you! As the Father has sent Me, I also send you.'"*

Sent one, sent into your sphere of influence. You are anointed to release the Kingdom through your life. Expect God to use you in your daily life. You are called to decree and release peace to the storms, chaos, and confusion. You are sent into your sphere of influence, anointed to share the gospel.

2121

Double Portion Wisdom to Walk in Maturity

21 often culturally represents a maturing, or coming of age. Stretching and growing into new maturity. Recalibration of the heart after God. Increased fear of the Lord. Double portion hunger and awareness of the season to seek God for upgraded wisdom. New maturity and authority in your call. Seek the Lord for wisdom as you humbly walk out this season. Pray and ask God for wisdom.

2022

Holy Spirit Power; Receive Divine Empowerment; Personal Pentecost and Anointing for the Season

John 20:22 NIV: *"And with that he breathed on them and said, 'Receive the Holy Spirit.'"*

God is anointing you with the power of His Holy Spirit. Expect upgrade. Receive supernatural empowerment for signs, wonders, and miracles as you release the Kingdom. Receive a fresh breath of life and personal Pentecost that anoints you for all God has called you to. Receive His power for the gospel and your call. Expect the power of God. Holy Spirit fire, impartation, and power encounters are increasing. Hunger for intimacy with His Holy Spirit, and refuse to do life and ministry without His empowerment.

3

333, 3333

Pray and Call on God and He Will Answer; Call to Prayer; Seek Him

Jeremiah 33:3 NIV: *"Call to me and I will answer you and tell you great and unsearchable things you do not know."*

Fresh revelation and divine strategy out of Heaven is being released. Pray. Ask and expect revelation and nearness of His presence; the unknown is available to be known; pray for the hidden to be revealed. Ask God for solutions. A call to intercession as hidden revelation is available to be received. A reminder God will answer you! Revelation for the path revealed. Expect encounter.

Ask of Him as He is releasing fresh, new revelation and strategy for the current season and circumstance. Expect divine answers.

316

You Are Loved; Release the Gospel; Salvation and Saving Grace

John 3:16 NIV: *"For God so loved the world that he gave his one and only Son, that whoever believes in him shall not perish but have eternal life."*

You are loved by God and have eternal life through salvation in Jesus. If you have not invited Jesus into your life as your Savior, then this is an invitation to you personally to invite Jesus into your life and be saved from eternity in hell and secure eternity in Heaven. This is a reminder that God loves you, and loves the world around you, and His heart is for them.

Ask the Lord what is His heart for those around you when you see this. Expect salvation encounters and release God's love for people. Look for those God is saying are "ripened harvest" and need the Lord.

Ask the Lord to show you the ripe harvest (people) in your midst. God wants to use you to share His heart and see the lost saved in your world. You are being reminded that you are called to be filled with the Holy Spirit and fire, and this is your inheritance. The Holy Spirit and fire are yours to help release the love of God as you go.

Walk in the power of the Holy Spirit and burning fire of God. As we are called into our sphere of influence, this is also a call to self-evaluate our "spiritual temperature." Are we hot and burning in our love for God and souls? Or are we lukewarm and complacent, and in need of fresh reviving? This is an invitation to stay burning for God and release God's love and fire to others. God wants to use you as His burning flame of love right where you are.

> Luke 3:16 NIV: *"John answered them all, 'I baptize you with water. But one who is more powerful than I will come, the straps of whose sandals I am not worthy to untie. He will baptize you with the Holy Spirit and fire.'"*
>
> Revelation 3:16 NKJV: *"So then, because you are lukewarm, and neither cold nor hot, I will vomit you out of My mouth."*

320

Make Room for Infinitely More; Expect More

> Ephesians 3:20 TPT: *"Never doubt God's mighty power to work in you and accomplish all this. He will achieve infinitely more than your greatest request, your most unbelievable dream, and exceed your wildest imagination! He will outdo them all, for his miraculous power constantly energizes you."*

Extend what you are believing for. Expand your faith. God is inviting you to dream with Him that there is "infinitely more" available and His miraculous power is available to walk in more. Let God stretch your heart and faith. Dream with God. God is doing more than you thought.

4

444, 4444

Double Doors for Victory; Increased Doors Opening; Creative Power for Breakthrough Present

> Psalm 44:4 NIV: *"You are my King and my God, who decrees victories for Jacob."*

Open door, double doors, creative miracles, creative opportunities opening, invitation to encounter fresh intimacy with God; come up higher, fresh perspective and increase of vision, breakthrough season of victory, decree God victories in your life.

The number 4 speaks of creation, the earth or creative works as the fourth day of creation saw material creation finished. In the Hebrew language the fourth letter is *dalet* and is represented pictorially as an open door, likened to an open tent door such as found entering the "tent of meeting." The open door implies an invitation to enter fresh, intimate encounter with God's presence and build intimacy with God. When seeing 4's take note of what you are doing at the time as it can be God talking of an open-door season and creative miracles, especially pertaining to entering the season you are on the threshold of. A fresh perspective as you come up higher and see the doors open to you. An increase of the seer gifting to see with greater clarity. God is decreeing victory over you. Align with what God is saying as you enter the door God has opened and decree victory. A call to decree and receive breakthrough in present situations.

> Revelation 4:1 NLT: *"Then as I looked, I saw a door standing open in heaven, and the same voice I had heard before spoke to me like a trumpet blast. The voice said, 'Come up here and I will show you what must happen after this.'"*

411

You're Called to Pour Out His Presence and Light; Awakening

> Zechariah 4:11-14 NIV: *"Then I asked the angel, 'What are these two olive trees on the right and the left of the lampstand?' Again I asked him, 'What are these two olive branches beside the two gold pipes that pour out golden oil?' He replied, 'Do you not know what these are?' "No, my lord,' I said. So he said, 'These are the two who are anointed to serve the Lord of all the earth.'"*

(These are the verses God gave my husband and I following a powerful angelic visitation and why we are called Pour It Out Ministries.)

Awakening. Awaken to His presence. A call to pour out oil and shine light in your sphere of influence and current circumstances. Whatever is going on around you, there's a reminder to give God the glory, honor and worthiness regardless of circumstances and receive and pour out the oil of his presence. Receive fresh oil. Pour out fresh oil. Give Him praise.

God is reminding us that He establishes authority in the church, and He gives us authority to walk in our call. Trust God to appoint you and honor Kingdom authority. Where God has you He is releasing fresh oil to revive you, and revive those you are called to. Seek the fresh oil of His presence and glory, and shine boldly. The fire on the lamp stand is kept burning by the crushing of the olives. The Lord is giving grace for fresh perspective that the crushing and pressure leads to fresh oil to burn with greater intensity.

> Ephesians 4:11 NKJV: *"And He Himself gave some to be apostles, some prophets, some evangelists, and some pastors and teachers,"*
>
> Revelation 4:11 NIV: *"You are worthy, our Lord and God, to receive glory and honor and power, for you created all things, and by your will they were created and have their being."*

414

Born for Such a Time as This; Anointed for Now

> Esther 4:14 NIV: *"For if you remain silent at this time, relief and deliverance for the Jews will arise from another place, but you and your father's family will perish. And who knows but that you have come to your royal position for such a time as this?"*

You are born for such a time as this. You are made for this season, and you are designed to excel in your gifts as you be the anointed version of you. Take courage and boldly be whom God has made you to be. Trust God to be courageous in all you are called to right now. The anointed, confidently bold version of you is more than able to step into the God dreams and God opportunities before you. Courageously speak and release the message you carry, and be confident that you are positioned in your sphere of influence for such a time as now.

Seek the Lord for favor and expect that your courageous influence will impact your sphere of influence. You are called, anointed, and appointed to your life for this exact moment. Trust that you carry God's presence and God is using you to release deliverance to hearts held captive. Steward your influence and make the most of the God opportunities you have. The dream in your heart may seem difficult or impossible, but believe that you are born for such a time as now and step out in courage. Your call is unique, needed, and purposed for now.

435

The Harvest Is Ripe; Take the Opportunities; Look for Souls

> John 4:35 NIV: *"Don't you have a saying, 'It's still four months until harvest'? I tell you, open your eyes and look at the fields! They are ripe for harvest."*

The harvest is ripe and ready in your sphere of influence. Seek the Lord for strategies now and expect God to use you now to win people for God, and see hearts turn to Jesus. There is a people or person ready for God right now. Don't put off what God is speaking to you about for another season; the field God has placed you in is ripe now. Ask God to open your eyes to what He is doing right now and allow Him to use you now. There are opportunities for revival harvest right now in your reach. Invite God to show you how He wants to use you and step out in courage.

5

555, 5555

Grace; His Abundant Grace

> Isaiah 55:1 NIV: *"Come, all you who are thirsty, come to the waters; and you who have no money, come, buy and eat! Come, buy wine and milk without money and without cost."*

Expect His grace on you and with you and around you. Five in the Bible most commonly symbolizes grace. Five can also signify favor and abundance. Abundant grace. Come to God and receive by grace. Come into His presence. Take notice of what you are talking about or doing when you see this. Grace to walk in the fullness of what you are called to, displaying His glory. Extend His grace on purpose.

> Isaiah 55:5 NIV: *"Surely you will summon nations you know not, and nations you do not know will come running to you, because of the Lord your God, the Holy One of Israel, for he has endowed you with splendor."*

6

66, 666

God Is Making a Way for You

> Psalm 66:6 NLT: *"He made a dry path through the Red Sea, and his people went across on foot. There we rejoiced in him."*

There are prophetic red seas that will open up before you so you can advance where it looked impossible to move forward. What looks impossible, God will make a way. Beginning praising God and decreeing the "red seas" that God has a way forward for you. Thank God He is still the God of breakthrough that parts red seas so His people can cross into promise. Believe for miraculous intervention. Decree God making a way for you.

Note: 666 is also the number used in the Bible to represent the arising of satan's power (anti-Christ) on the earth, and can speak to discerning evil agenda. However, many immediately jump to feeling fearful when they have seen this number. I love Psalm 66:6 as it speaks to God pushing back the enemy's attacks and supernaturally making a way of breakthrough. God is evicting fear in Jesus' name associated to your circumstances, stirring faith that God is with you and making a way. God is bigger than the circumstance.

7

77, 777

Completion and Fullness

Proverbs 6:31 NKJV: *"Yet when he [the thief] is found, he must restore sevenfold...."*

Completion, fullness, restoration, wholeness. God will complete what He has promised. Entering into the promises of God. God is revealing pathways of breakthrough that have previously been unseen. God is revealing previously hidden pathways of breakthrough. The hidden pathways of breakthrough are being revealed. Where the road ahead has been hidden or blocked, God is revealing the way forward. Prophetic red seas are parting to bring about advance/promise.

Sevenfold (perfected) Divine Restitution. A paying back of what the enemy " has stolen. A promise of full restoration. God is promising complete restoration and restitution; however, allow Him to do this His way and surrender to His plan over our plans.

Ask, seek, and knock. Persistence in prayer. What you seek in the Kingdom, you find. Seek the Lord in prayer. God is using your prayers to bring restoration of promise and breakthrough.

Psalm 77:19 NLT: *"Your road led though the sea, your pathway through the mighty waters—a pathway no one knew was there!"*

Matthew 7:7 NIV: *"Ask and it will be given to you; seek and you will find; knock and the door will be opened to you."*

737

Drink in God's Presence; Focus on Jesus; Receive From His Presence

John 7:37 NIV: *"...Jesus stood and said in a loud voice, 'Let anyone who is thirsty come to me and drink.'"*

Drink of God's presence! Focus on God's presence and worship the Lord because He is near. God has refreshing in His presence for you right now, but a deliberate purposed decision to focus on Him is required to receive. Take time to drink in God's goodness in a set-apart way. Consider where you are and what season you are in when you see this. Are you dry, dull, or disconnected from God? It's time to seek the Lord even if it means pushing past the noise of the crowd and life. There is an invitation for Jesus Himself to minister to you in new intimacy as you pursue His heart above complacency and distractions. This is a call to press into radical heart encounters with God.

747

Take-Off Season; Higher Perspective

A take-off season, of destiny, influence and/or promise. God is taking you higher and farther. Expansion. Increase of influence. A "taking off" and rocketing into the now promises over your life. A call to higher perspective and revelation that can only come through new emphasis on strategic prayer and declaration.

It can be specifically referencing travel and flying (as in a 747 plane, but this can just mean expansion and going higher) and/or increase of influence. As influence expands, new authority is established with the intention of releasing Heaven on earth with an upgraded power-punch in your area of influence.

A call to go up higher and prioritize prophetic intercession where clarity will be given through purposed prayer focus. It is implied that to go farther you must go higher. You are entering a new season that requires increased emphasis on prayer and revelatory wisdom that comes only from a higher perspective in Him. Clarity will return as you are taken up higher. The mountains will be defeated as divine strategy is released in prayer.

You are being taken into a new season that requires a new strategy.

748

Take the Next Step Into the New Season
Expansion on expansion. You are going higher!

8

888, 88

New Beginnings
There are fresh, new beginnings springing up from the ashes. Thank God for a fresh wind blowing, and new

possibilities opening up in your life. God is equally calling you to wipe the slate clean in your heart, to "let the captives free from your heart" and allow for fresh hope of new life. Ask the Lord to highlight anything that is keeping you tethered to a past place of pain or old-wineskin thinking, and embrace the new thing God is doing in you. Look for what God is doing and embrace the new.

818

You Are a Sign and Wonder of His Glory on Display to This Generation

Expect beginning of life, wealth creation and establishment of promise. New beginnings of life in circumstances that have seemed without hope or fresh life. A re-boot of life where the enemy has tried to rob hope from you.

> Isaiah 8:18 TPT: *"Behold—here I stand, and the children whom the Lord Yahweh has given me are for signs and wonders in Israel, sent from the Lord Almighty, Commander of Angel Armies, who is enthroned on Mount Zion!"*

You are a sign and a wonder sent from the Lord Almighty, Commander of Angel Armies, to this generation.

> Deuteronomy 8:18 NKJV: *"And you shall remember the Lord your God, for it is He who gives you power to get wealth, that He may establish His covenant which He swore to your fathers, as it is this day."*

God is giving you the power to create wealth and establish promise.

> Romans 8:18 TPT: *"I am convinced that any suffering we endure is less than nothing compared to the magnitude of glory that is about to be unveiled within us."*

The glory is increasing upon you.

You have a glorious destiny that outweighs the suffering.

You are a sign and wonder of His glory on display to this generation.

18, 1818

Decree Life; Bind and Release in Prayer

> Matthew 18:18 NIV: *"Truly I tell you, whatever you bind on earth will be bound in heaven, and whatever you loose on earth will be loosed in heaven."*

Decree life and allow the Lord to upgrade your faith to believe for life to infuse your situations and circumstance, where the enemy has tried to speak hopelessness. God has given you authority to shift the atmosphere and circumstance. Use your voice and authority to bind the agenda of the darkness, and release the Kingdom's agenda. A call to battle in the heavenlies; evict the enemy's plans and speak forth God's promises. Release the promises of God in intercession. Speak life. Use your authority in prayer.

9

99, 999

Fruitfulness and Harvest

Harvest of seeds faithfully sown, harvest of souls, the value of one soul, fruitfulness. As one season comes to an end, make room for the new. Finality of one season. 9 o'clock in the morning was "happy hour" when His Spirit was poured out and Jesus' disciples were accused of being drunk when they were filled with the power and joy of the Holy Spirit. This encourages me that the finality of one season is the beginning of a new season—and look for Holy Spirit power and joy to empower you.

> Matthew 18:12 NLT: *"If a man has a hundred sheep and one of them wanders away, what will he do? Won't he leave the ninety-nine others on the hills and go out to search for the one that is lost?"*
>
> Acts 2:15 NIV: *"These people are not drunk, as you suppose. It is only nine in the morning!"*

911

Urgent Call to Prayer; Decree Psalm 91 Protection, Angelic Protection

> Psalm 91:11 NIV: *"For he will command his angels concerning you to guard you in all your ways;"*

Urgency in the spirit. Pray. A call to prayer and a call to decree what Heaven is releasing as opposed to what darkness is trying to release. An urgency and grace for intercession. Angelic protection. Restoration of Kingdom objectives. A call to decree restoration and rebuilding of God's design. Take note what you are talking about or planning when you see this. Pray and call forth what God is saying and not what the enemy is pushing for. A personal call to intercession.

911 is a call to stand on Psalm 91 and declare God's peace and protection in times of high alertness in the spirit. Angelic protection. God has sent His angelic host to surround you and the assignment He has given you. Lean into peace and not fear. This is a call to offensive prayer, with the promise of Psalm 91 as a shield of protection and peace.

Peace be with you. Restoration of promise, rebuilding of God's original intention, repair, and healing of brokenness and repairing of broken Kingdom structures, strategies and connections; life being revived from ruins; a rising up of a house and people known for worship and passionate devotion to the Lord; a raising up of a people that worship the Lord as David did leading to radical revival and reformation. Again, a call to decree and pray.

All of Psalm 91. Read and decree this over you, your family, and your nation.

> Amos 9:11 NLT: *"In that day I will restore the fallen house of David. I will repair its damaged walls. From the ruins I will rebuild it and restore its former glory."*

912

God Will Do This; Restoration of God's Purposes

Amos 9:12 NLT: *"And Israel will possess what is left of Edom and all the nations I have called to be mine. The Lord has spoken, and he will do these things."*

Pray and decree "God will do this." An establishing of season from restoration and rebuilding into possession, dominion and new authority over spiritual territory. Continue to pray and step into what God is decreeing. A continuation of Amos 9:11 into Amos 9:12 where restoration leads to possession of the promise. God establishes He will do this! The restoration process is leading to greater spiritual authority. Transition from chaos into restoration of God's purpose and promise.

10

1010

Abundant Life; Speak Life to the Full

John 10:10 NIV: *"The thief comes only to steal and kill and destroy; I have come that they may have life, and have it to the full."*

Order, completion of order, fullness of a season. Where the enemy brought destruction, God is releasing life and speaking fullness of life. An invitation to decree fullness of life in circumstances. God's promise of abundant life. A call to bind the enemy's attacks and release the fullness of the Kingdom into circumstances.

11

1111

Awakening and Resurrection Power (See the section on 11:11 and under "1" for 111/1111.)

1112

Transition Into God's Order

> Deuteronomy 11:12 NIV: *"It is a land the Lord your God cares for; the eyes of the Lord your God are continually on it from the beginning of the year to its end."*

Transition into apostolic order and government. A new breed. Changing of the guard. Promotion. A shifting into a new alignment. Stepping into new anointing for the new season.

God's faithfulness and careful attention to watch over you from beginning to end of the season you are in. Nothing escapes His care.

12

1212

Divine Order; Kingdom Governmental Rule

Divine order; apostolic government and fullness; Kingdom government; perfect rule. A season coming into Kingdom completion and order. A stepping into right order. An upgrade and shifting into Kingdom, governmental order around you.

1234

Alignment; God is Lining Everything Up for You

Alignment. "I'm lining everything up for you, as easy as ABC, 1234."—God

Divine alignment and positioning. God is lining things up for you with ease. God is watching over you. You can trust Him. When you see God, you will find Him. You can trust God for the next step. When God is your treasure, your heart runs hard after Him. Make God the highest treasure in your life.

> *Luke 12:34 NIV: "Where your treasure is, there your heart will be also."*

1235

Take the Next Step; Be Ready; Burn for Jesus

> Luke 12:35 NIV: *"Be dressed ready for service and keep your lamps burning."*

Take the next step. There is a grace to step into what God is speaking to you about. God is aligning things for expansion and extending the borders of your faith. Get dressed and ready to run. Don't put off for tomorrow what God is speaking to you about for today—this season.

God is calling His bride from lukewarm to hot. An upgraded anointing for service and to be *burning ones*. Wait in His presence until you are burning and get oil to keep going. It is an urgent invitation to come into the secret place, fall in love all over again, and receive from Him what you need for this *now* season. Prioritize Him now, not later, as burning ones are marked for service. God is asking, "Are you ready?"

Jesus desires a bride who burns for Him. Jesus, like any "husband" desires to be loved above "other things" by His bride. You are being called into more, marked by fire and anointed to burn. May you sense His wooing and know God loves you deeply. Be ready.

12345, 2345

Take the next step. It's time for the next step.

Birthday or Birth Time; Your Birthday; Your Birth Date or Year; Your Time of Birth, etc.; God Knows You, Sees You, and Loves You; You Are Born for Such a Time as This

> Psalm 139:13-17 TPT: *"You formed my innermost being, shaping my delicate inside and my intricate outside, and wove them all together in my mother's womb. I thank you, God, for making me so mysteriously complex! Everything you do is marvelously breathtaking. It simply amazes me to think about it! How thoroughly you know me, Lord! You even formed every bone in my body when you created me in the secret place, carefully, skillfully shaping me from nothing to something. You saw who you created me to be before I became me! Before I'd ever seen the light of day, the number of days you planned for me were already recorded in your book. Every single moment you are thinking of me! How precious and wonderful to consider that you cherish me constantly in your every thought!..."*

THE KING'S PROPHETIC VOICE

You are loved, seen, and known fully by Father God. There is a God dream and purpose for your life, and God is blessing you to live in the days that He desires for you. God is speaking about how precious you are to Him. You are never alone, you are never unloved. You are uniquely made and anointed to walk in breath-taking promise and with heart-fulfilling destiny. Every day of your life is precious, and God keeps a record of your life and celebrates you and is creating days of purpose for you. You have a hope and future that is good (as Jeremiah 29:11 says). The Lord is inviting you to know that there are things on earth that only you can do and be, and He loves celebrating you fulfilling the desires of your heart as you enjoy His love of you. Every day has purpose and every day you are loved. You are truly born for such a time as this, and God cherishes you.

> Esther 4:14 NKJV: *"Yet who knows whether you have come to the kingdom for such a time as this?"*
>
> Jeremiah 29:11 NIV: *"For I know the plans I have for you,' declares the Lord, 'plans to prosper you and not to harm you, plans to give you hope and a future.'"*

Doubles and Multiples; Double Portion

For example: 316:316; 911911; 44444444; 747747, 88888888888—you keep seeing double of the same number, doubles or multiples of everything, or number combinations at the same time.

> Isaiah 61:7 NIV: *"Instead of your shame you will receive a double portion, and instead of disgrace you will rejoice*

in your inheritance. And so you will inherit a double portion in your land, and everlasting joy will be yours."

Double portion reward for you and increase. Thank the Lord for double for your trouble. Expect increase and invite God to expand what you are believing for, walking in and trusting Him for. Thank the Lord that He restores double. There's a multiplying of God's power at work in your life. God is emphasizing the message of whatever that number combination means.

Sequences

Lining it All Up 211, 311, 411, 511, 611, 711, 811

When seen in sequence or with great regularity, it often is a reminder that God is lining things up and bringing things into correct order. Alignment for a move of His Spirit. A time of strategic transition into His promises. A countdown in the Spirit. A call to decree His purposes.

Transition

247, 347, 447, 547, 647, 747, 847, 947

When seen regularly and in sequence it can be referring to a count down in the Spirit of all that "747" means. Higher and farther. Increase. God is taking you on a journey of specific strategic steps that will bring increase. Take the next step. Put plans in place to enter into a season of prayer and expansion, and do what God directs. The clear air provided by prophetic intercession is needed in this season of expansion.

Combinations Accelerating Upward

1122, 1133, 1144, etc.

This speaks of acceleration and double portion increase. That things are happening fast. God is with you in the process of acceleration.

IMPORTANT NOTE

The Pour It Out Ministries Number Sequence Prophetic Meaning Guide is not an exhaustive list or study. It can be used as a springboard into praying and seeking God for yourself in what He is saying to you. This is a work in progress, as it's an ongoing conversation with the Lord. These are my discoveries so far and what I have found are by far the most common numbers people see.

Of course, as this is a personal conversation between you and God, what a number means in one season to you, may shift or expand into more in another season. I encourage you to keep seeking the Lord for further meaning and insight, especially if you haven't found the number you're looking for listed here.

I hope this is helpful to you, and I welcome your feedback, and stories of what God has said to you. I have discovered that as soon as you embark on translating the King's prophetic voice for yourself, it's contagious and brings ever-increasing revelation, joy, and connection to God. I'm excited for all you will discover. Be blessed as God speaks to you.

Jodie Hughes

Pour It Out Ministries

Find us at pouritout.org

ABOUT THE AUTHOR

Jodie Hughes and her husband, Ben, are the founders of Pour It Out Ministries and hosts of Pour It Out TV. They have been in ministry together for more than 20 years. They, along with their adult daughter Keely, travel full time around the world as revivalists, with an emphasis on revival and evangelism, breakthrough, prophetic declaration, healing, and preaching of the gospel, with miracles, signs, and wonders following in their personal lives and ministry.

They also have a powerful television and media ministry, reaching millions of homes around the world on a weekly basis through their own TV shows on GOD TV and Sid Roth's ISN Network, among many others. (See www.pouritout.tv for archives.)

Jodie and her family are known for hosting the Pineapple Revival in Australia that saw many thousands come from all over, extending for 18 months. As well as being full-time itinerant revivalists, they have pastored and planted several churches, trained thousands of ministry students in their schools, recorded worship albums, and both have authored books and various prophetic articles and blogs.

Jodie is an engaging speaker and influencer known for being real, inspiring hope, and imparting contagious hunger and transferable revival fire.

Ministry Contact Information:

https://www.pouritout.org

Made in the USA
Coppell, TX
06 December 2023

25453409R00177